PLAYING **BIG**

Tara Mohr is the founder of the global Playing Big leadership programme for women and an expert on women's leadership and well-being: her '10 Rules for Brilliant Women' was a viral sensation. Trained by the Coaches Training Institute, Tara also holds an MBA from Stanford University and a degree in English literature from Yale. She is a regular contributor to the *Huffington Post*, in demand as a key-note speaker – at the Emerging Women Live conference, and for TEDx, The White House Project and Harvard Business School – and has been featured on the *Today* show, *Forbes Woman*, *Harvard Business Review*, *Financial Times*, the BBC and numerous other media outlets.

To find out more about Tara Mohr and *Playing Big*, visit:
www.taramohr.com.

Follow Tara on Twitter: @TaraSophia

PLAYING **BIG**

A practical guide
for brilliant women like you

TARA MOHR

arrow books

1 3 5 7 9 10 8 6 4 2

Arrow Books
20 Vauxhall Bridge Road
London SW1V 2SA

Arrow Books is part of the Penguin Random House group of companies whose
addresses can be found at global.penguinrandomhouse.com.

Penguin
Random House
UK

Quotation from Lisa Jemus on pages 26–27 courtesy of Lisa Jemus. Quotation from Kellie
McElhaney on pages 27–28 courtesy of Kellie McElhaney, a professor at UC Berkeley's Haas School
of Business. Quotation from Sandy Johnson Clark on pages 41–42 courtesy of Sandy Johnson Clark,
an executive at a career management firm. Quotation from Gerd Nilsson on page 49 courtesy of Gerd
Nilsson. The "Future Self Guided Visualization" on pages 54–58 courtesy of the Coaches Training
Institute. Quotation from Barbara Wasserman on page 68 courtesy of Barbara Wasserman, a therapist
and coach. Quotation from Erin Geesaman Rabke on page 70 courtesy of Erin Geesaman Rabke.
Quotation from Diana Tedoldi on page 71 courtesy of Diana Tedoldi. Quotation from Meeta Kaur
on pages 103–104 courtesy of Meeta Kaur, a speaker on Sikh American women and the creator of a
collection of Sikh American women's writings. Quotation from Carol Anne Wall on pages 158–159
courtesy of Carol Anne Wall, a reporting analyst and adjunct writing professor. Quotation from
Stacey Sargeant on pages 159–160 courtesy of Stacey Sargeant, leadership and team development
expert. Quotation from Laura Grisolano on pages 167–168 courtesy of Laura Grisolano, president,
Bridge Mediation & Dispute Resolution Services LLC. Quotation from Melissa Dinwiddie on page
171 courtesy of Melissa Dinwiddie, artist and creativity coach. Quotations from Jeena Cho on pages
213–214 courtesy of Jeena Cho, author of *The Anxious Lawyer*. Quotations on pages 227 and 236
from *The Willpower Instinct: How Self-Control Works, Why It Matters, and What You Can Do to Get
More of It* by Kelly McGonigal, copyright © 2012 by Kelly McGonigal, PhD. Used by permission of
Macmillan Publishing Ltd.

First published by Hutchinson in 2014

First published in the US by Gotham Books
Published by arrangement with Gotham Books, a member of Penguin Group (USA) LLC,
a Penguin Random House Company

First published in paperback by Arrow Books in 2015

www.randomhouse.co.uk

A CIP catalogue record for this book is available from the British Library.

ISBN 9780099591528

Printed and bound by CPI Group (UK) Ltd, Croydon, CR0 4YY

MIX
Paper from
responsible sources
FSC
www.fsc.org   FSC® C018179

Penguin Random House is committed to a sustainable future
for our business, our readers and our planet. This book is
made from Forest Stewardship Council® certified paper.

FOR HARRIET AND BILL

CONTENTS

• • •

INTRODUCTION

· · ·

You know that woman. She's a good friend or a colleague from work. She's smart and insightful. She gets it: Whatever the situation at her company, or in her community, or in the news, she has great ideas about what needs to happen. She's high integrity too—no greed, no temptation to corruption, no big hunger for power. And she's funny, warm, and trustworthy.

Sometimes, you listen to her talk and think, if only people like her were in charge . . .

So here's the thing: The way that you look at that woman? Someone looks at you that way. In fact, many people do. To us, *you* are that talented woman who doesn't see how talented she is. You are the woman who—it's clear to us—could start an innovative company or pull one out of the dysfunction it's in, improve the local schools, or write a book that would change thousands of lives. You are that fabulous, we-wish-she-was-speaking-up-more woman.

Playing Big is about bridging the gap between what we see in you and what you know about yourself. It's a practical guide to moving past self-doubt and creating what you most want to create—whether in your career, in your community, or in a passion you pursue outside of work. It's not about the old-school notion of playing big—more money, more prestigious title, a bigger empire, or fame. It's about you living with a sense of greater freedom to express your voice and pursue your aspirations. It's playing big according to what playing big truly means to you. And if you don't know what playing big looks like for you yet, the ideas and tools here will help you discover that.

This playing big is not about climbing the ladder within broken systems. It's about learning how to use your voice to change those systems. It's not about "opting in" or "opting out" according to our society's current thinking around what women should and shouldn't be doing. It's about turning away from those narrow labels, refocusing your attention on your longings and dreams, and playing big in going for them.

This book was born out of a frustration and a hope. The frustration? Brilliant women are playing small. The hope? That the world could be changed—for the much, much better—by our greater participation.

Nisha was one of my first coaching clients: in her early thirties; long, flowing black hair; always in bright colors that brought to life her beautiful face. Nisha was a midlevel program manager at a nonprofit organization. She was known there as a quiet, organized administrator, good at implementing others' plans.

Yet in our coaching sessions, I got to know a very different Nisha. It turned out she was an avid learner who spent much of her free time reading the important journals and books related to her field. She was a creative thinker, full of ideas for how her organization could improve its work by incorporating the latest thinking in the industry. I happened to be very familiar with Nisha's employer and, after just a few meetings with her, could see that she was thinking about the future of the organization in a way that was at least as sophisticated and smart, if not more so, as the CEO and board were. But no one in Nisha's workplace knew any of this. Nisha's ideas and gifts were hidden. They were not making it out of her head and heart and into her organization.

Among my coaching clients, friends, and colleagues, I kept encountering women like Nisha: brilliant women who couldn't quite see their own brilliance, women who were convinced their ideas needed more perfecting or refinement or time before being put into action, or women who—for reasons they weren't sure of—were not moving forward toward their greatest aspirations and dreams. It bothered me, a lot, because I wanted to live in the better, more humane, more enlightened world I knew these women could create.

There was Elizabeth, another client, a dynamic former magazine editor who had adopted four children from abroad. She wanted to write about her experiences of adopting. "Tara," she said to me, "I feel like I've learned so much about what motherhood is really about and what life is all about. Yet everything I know and have learned from the past years of raising these children—well, when I look out into the world, it's like it's invisible. No one is talking about it." I read Elizabeth's blog posts—essays she wrote quickly in between carpool shifts and swimming lessons. Her writing was powerful, and she was indeed talking about motherhood and love across borders in new and important ways. I wanted to see her perspective in newspaper op-eds and on bookstore shelves. And yet despite Elizabeth's many connections in the publishing industry, she was stuck—held back both by bouts of insecurity and by a sense of overwhelm and confusion about the practical steps to take.

And then there was Cynthia. Cynthia was a director of sales at a Silicon Valley tech company. Super sharp and hardworking, Cynthia also had an incredible gift for mediating conflict. But Cynthia was relatively bored in her job—having worked in the same kind of role for over a decade and never having enjoyed it much to begin with. There was, however, another arena of the company's work that she was excited about, exploring a new line of business she felt could be very successful and bring customers a valuable new service. When we talked about Cynthia pitching to the senior leadership that they invest in such a position and put her in it, she couldn't believe *she'd* be able to get that kind of special opportunity.

Each of these women had the potential to be shaping her organizations and communities in a much more significant way than she was. Each had the talent, intelligence, and training to easily achieve the dream that felt out of reach. And each one was missing out on a lot of joy, fulfillment, and professional success as a result. I believe that most of us are in some way like these women—not seeing how possible our big dreams are, not seeing our own capabilities, and not yet having careers as successful, easeful, and exhilarating as we could.

I was personally frustrated by what I was observing in my clients. Nisha had powerful ideas and critiques that could help move her organization forward. Cynthia was the kind of dedicated, ethical, collaborative leader we need more of in the corporate world. Elizabeth's writings about service and mothering told an important story too hidden in our cultural conversation. I wanted to see these kinds of brilliant women and their ideas impacting our world. So for me, the question of how to get their voices out was personally urgent. It was also professionally urgent, because they were coming to me for help.

My coaching practice became a laboratory to discover: What would enable these women to create the careers and lives they really wanted? In coaching sessions, the rubber meets the road. It's not enough to give advice that sounds good; together with the client, you've got to *produce the change* that the client is seeking.

I needed to figure out: What had to happen so that Nisha could become a respected leader in her organization? So that Elizabeth's writing would reach people beyond her friends and family? So that Cynthia could do work that energized her each day?

There are the conventional answers: more confidence, good mentors, some accountability around the steps toward their goals. I quickly learned by working with clients that none of those things helped much. Tactics and tips—how to write a résumé, interview, negotiate, speak in front of a group—didn't do the job, because women couldn't use all that new knowledge if the inner foundation for taking risks, overcoming fears, and dealing with self-doubt wasn't in place. Helping women develop relationships with mentors was mostly ineffectual, because without the tools to trust their own thinking and be discerning about mentors' advice, they'd get lost in others' opinions and depart from the course that was truly right for them. The conventional supports didn't go deep enough; they didn't get to what was holding women back or what they needed to move forward.

What *did* help women play bigger was a set of concepts and practices that changed how they thought about themselves and the kind of action they took. It was a set of movements—away from listening to the voice of self-doubt within and instead listening to a voice of calm and wisdom; away from perfectionism and overplanning and toward a new way of taking quick action; away from worrying about what other people thought and toward a focus on their own fulfillment; away from self-discipline and toward self-care. All those pieces worked together to create an inner infrastructure that supported women to go for their dreams boldly, to both overcome internal blocks and better deal with external challenges.

The same set of tools and practices helped diverse women play bigger: young women and older ones, corporate women and start-up entrepreneurs, women in business, the social sector, and the arts. After a few years of coaching women, I took the work I'd been doing with my clients and created a group experience, a leadership program called Playing Big. From its first session, it received rave reviews. Today, over one thousand women from around the world have participated in the program. Some have applied the work to playing big in high-powered careers, others to a pursuit outside of work, like a creative passion or volunteer activity. I'm proud that participants report that as a result of the program, they

- feel more confident.
- share their unique ideas, questions, and critiques more frequently and more boldly.
- are less afraid of criticism.
- are more powerful communicators.
- can tap into their inner wisdom more easily.
- feel a greater sense that they have and are "enough" to do what they want to do in their careers.
- see themselves as a part of a global network of women seeking to make positive change.
- are playing bigger according to what playing bigger means to them.

As a result of those inner changes, they've made the career moves they desired, received promotions and raises, launched and grown their businesses, and taken on leadership roles. They started changing their communities—and the world—in the ways they longed to but didn't think they could before. In this book, you'll learn what they learned so that you can walk your own path to playing bigger.

My Story

In some sense, this book began its journey into being more than twenty years ago. I was a fifteen-year-old, short-shorts wearing, Red Hot Chili Peppers–loving, wannabe rebel teenage girl. On the first day of a new school year, I waited through chemistry lab (nothing could have bored me more), Spanish class (so-so, I thought), precalculus (hated it), and, worst of all, P.E. to get to the promised land: *English class*. English class: the realm of characters and stories and poems and big ideas—everything I loved.

Little did I know I was about to be very disappointed.

Our teacher gave his first-day-of-school introductory speech, leaning against a decaying metal desk with his arms folded and resting on his big belly. "This year we'll explore the theme of 'Coming-of-Age'—the transition from childhood to adulthood. We'll read diverse stories of coming-of-age: *Black Boy* by Richard Wright, *A Separate Peace* by John Knowles, *Lord of the Flies* by William Golding. We'll uncover the universal themes and challenges around this rite of passage."

At first, I just noticed that I didn't feel very excited about any of the books. Then I realized why. *None* of the books were about a girl coming-of-age. At fifteen years old I knew that girls' coming-of-age and boys' coming-of-age made for very different tales. I wanted a story I could relate to.

Then I noticed none of the books were written by women either. I thought to myself, here was this grown-up telling me we were going to learn about this subject fully, while we were really hearing only male voices. I knew, even at fifteen, that my English class was not the only place like this. In a thousand ways in my life, I could see, boys' and men's stories were being told as the whole story.

I felt a kind of pang in my chest and a rush of energy. I knew I had to do something about this. I went over to the teacher's desk after class. "Mr. Haverson? Um, I wanted to ask you about something. I noticed that none of the books are by women, and none of them are about girls coming of age. It seems . . . unbalanced."

"These are the books we have. I don't have the budget to purchase any other books," he told me.

"Well, how could we raise the money?" I heard myself ask back.

Within months, a committee had been formed, a few thousand dollars raised, and a curriculum plan approved. The following year, new books written by women and featuring female protagonists were added to a number of English classes taught at the school.

That was the beginning of what has become a lifelong calling for me: to recognize where women's voices are missing and do what I can, in my corner of the world, to help bring them in.

After high school, I went off to Yale and experienced in a different way how women's voices were missing. Large portraits of the school's leaders graced the walls, but those portraits were never of women. The tenured faculty was mostly male, and none of the books required for English majors to read—not one—was written by a woman. Whenever someone got up to give a speech to the student body, it wasn't someone who looked like me. Women were new arrivals—present for only thirty of the school's nearly three-hundred-year history. They had been allowed to join the institution and participate in it, but there had been no inquiry into how to significantly adapt the institution so that women and men would thrive equally there.

When I graduated from college, I teamed up with two other women to create an anthology of Jewish women's writings about the Passover holiday, enabling families to add women's perspectives to a liturgy that—despite being about freedom and oppression—traditionally included no women's voices.

A few years later, I surprised my friends and family by deciding that my next move would be to get an MBA. I wasn't the typical business school candidate, but I was eager to learn the tools to grow mission-driven organizations to significant scale. Stanford Business School allowed me to do just that. It also gave me a kind of crash course on the culture surrounding women in the corporate world—a culture which all too often resembles that of a frat house. At both Yale and Stanford, I saw very clearly that it's simply not enough for institutions created by and for men to open their doors to women. Much more needs to change—the norms, the practices, and the face of its leadership—to create a place where women can truly succeed.

In all those experiences, I found myself longing for an environment more equally shaped by women and men. And there was a second kind of change I wanted to see as well: that all the expertise about the external world these institutions had to offer would become integrated with wisdom about our inner lives, the internal reality that shaped external events.

I had an unusual childhood. I was seven years old before I learned that not all children analyzed their dreams each morning at the breakfast table with mom and dad, diagramming the archetypes on a yellow pad, next to the bowl of oatmeal. When I came home with a childhood complaint like "Johnny teased me at recess," I was usually met with "What do you think is going on at home for Johnny that would cause him to tease other kids?"

My parents weren't psychotherapists, religious fanatics, or even hippies. They were regular people who believed that understanding oneself and others was an essential part of living a happy life. From an early age, I was encouraged to learn about psychology and spirituality from all traditions—Eastern and Western—and apply tools from both areas to my daily life. Our house was full of books on those subjects and I grew up reading them. By the time I was a teenager, I was attending spiritual retreats and hanging out in the psychology section of the bookstore in my free time. I used meditation, journaling, and therapy to help me survive the storm of adolescence—and they helped, a lot.

In a thousand ways, my parents taught me that what happens in our inner lives shapes our outer realities. At the same time, I navigated a very different landscape: *school*. At home I was being told all human beings were equally miraculous creations of the divine, but at school there was a lot of ranking of kids, classes for the "gifted" children and, therefore, the presumably not-gifted ones. At home I was taught that people's inner lives and unconscious motivations drive their behavior, but the teachers' lessons on presidents and prime ministers certainly never discussed their inner lives. I couldn't figure out why at school we weren't talking about how Lincoln's early childhood impacted his decisions, or why we never discussed the underlying psychological dynamics that led to every escalation to war.

Throughout my childhood, I often felt that I was living with one foot in each of two very different worlds. One world was about thinking, the other about emotion. One was about knowledge, the other about intuition. One was about what we can see and touch and hear, the other was about the inner life that created that tangible reality.

As I sought to weave together these two worlds, I moved between what I'd now call times of playing big and times of playing small. During some periods, I could remember what I truly loved—writing, the arts, spirituality, entrepreneurship, creativity, women's empowerment, and being a part of a community—and I could build a life that was about those things. But during many years, I was lost from all that. My education helped develop my intellect, but the artist in me became lost along the way and I neglected my spiritual life. I became a bit cynical about personal growth work, taking my cues from the academic culture around me rather than listening inward to what I knew to be true. Worst of all, I developed some fabulous "critical thinking" skills but then applied them to my own dreams for my future, playing the skeptic instead of being an ally to myself.

In my early thirties, I started to feel a disconnect from self that felt too painful to ignore, and I entered a process of significantly changing my life so that it reflected my real aspirations, both for my life and for my work. I also began to look closely at my own self-doubt and find my path to a more confident way of moving through the world. Many of the tools that helped me became tools I later used with my female coaching clients and in my leadership programs for women—tools now included in this book.

Helping Women Play Bigger

After business school, I went to work at a major foundation with two billion dollars in assets. One of the things I loved about the foundation, and one of the reasons I'd taken the job there, was its many strong women leaders. Nearly every part of the foundation was run by a talented, hardworking woman. But the very top position of CEO had been held only by men for the one hundred years of the organization's existence.

While I was there, a new CEO was brought in. He was a young man who didn't have experience managing large organizations but had a great deal of talent, charisma, and potential. Over the months that followed, his newly hired team launched major new initiatives quickly, without much research, testing, or planning, and allocated major dollars to them. The senior women who had been slowly rising in the ranks as they painstakingly gained more experience were overruled and passed over for promotions. On more than one occasion I heard those senior men ridicule the hardest working of those women as having no personal lives and call those who were most resistant to their decisions "difficult."

I was stunned, and I was learning. I watched men move massive amounts of money and see their projects realized—even though they hadn't done much homework on them—while highly qualified women with important ideas to share stood on the sidelines both because they weren't listened to and because they didn't feel those ideas were ready for prime time.

Growing up in the eighties and nineties, I had been told that women had equal opportunity in the workplace now, that young women like me had nothing to worry about, that if anything still stood in the way of women's career advancement, it was only the inevitable tension between work and family. Yet what I saw happening at my workplace was something else entirely—something that had to do with power, bias, confidence, and risk-taking.

As I talked with friends about what was occurring at my organization, I heard similar stories, again and again, about theirs: stories about charismatic male leaders at the helm, men who made bold but often rash decisions. Their organizations too were full of talented, hardworking women in lieutenant and other senior roles. Those women worked longer hours, were more attuned to the details, and had more experience and knowledge. Yet they were not leading at the highest levels, both because they were not being put in positions of leadership and because they weren't sharing audacious ideas or initiating big plans. Their employers were utilizing their strong work ethic but not their brilliance—their unique ideas, insights, and talents.

While I loved many aspects of my work in philanthropy—my colleagues, applying my MBA education to a social mission, and working with inspiring philanthropists—after a few years, I started to have the sense that it was not what I wanted to do long-term. I faced the truth that many of the real dreams I had for my career—to do something highly creative, entrepreneurial, and in the personal growth field—had gotten buried during my time in college and graduate school.

I'd been exposed to the field of coaching while at Stanford Business School and was intrigued. Coaching was a way to work with people's inner lives but with a focus on action and impact. That was just what I was looking for. I got trained as a coach and I also started blogging about personal growth. For a couple of years, my life looked like this: wake up at five; write a blog post; jump on the train; go to work at the foundation all day; and then, around six, head over to the office that I rented for a handful of hours each week to meet with my coaching clients.

It was around this time that I started to notice again and again brilliant women around me playing small. I first saw it in my clients, women like Nisha, Elizabeth, and Cynthia. I also saw it in my friends. One day, I was on a Saturday-morning walk with three of my girlfriends. I listened as Jessa talked about what she thought needed to be done to fix the dysfunctional school board in her kids' district. I listened as Britt talked about some questionable practices happening in her company. I listened as Abby told the most remarkable story about a game she'd created for her nieces and nephews to help them learn about their family history. I listened as the whole group shared their sorrows and hopes about the news headlines of the week. I listened to them talk, in awe of their intelligence, their ideas, and their character—their honest concern for others and their commitment to doing the right thing. I kept thinking, *these* are the kind of people I wish were in charge: hardworking, wise, ethical women and men who care a great deal about people.

I said something along those lines—that I wished Jessa would join her school board, that Britt would get into a leadership role at her company, that Abby would write a book about parenting. They chuckled in response to my suggestions. They thought of themselves as amateurs pontificating, not as people whose ideas were ready for a larger stage.

Then the thought struck me: On that particular Saturday morning, around the country, there were *thousands* of groups like ours—women walking and talking about what was wrong with the status quo, what was needed, women sharing alternative visions of how things could be. Those ideas and critiques were being left on the sidewalks and trails, heard only in intimate conversations among friends. Leaps of imagination, important ideas and questions, and visions for change were not making it to the bigger stages where they could be heard and where they were desperately needed.

Of course, I was so attuned to this phenomenon of women playing small because I was struggling with it myself. All the support, education, and success I'd had somehow had not added up to confidence. It hadn't left me eager to pursue my dreams. Instead I was petrified of failure, embarrassment, not being good enough. As a result, I was not doing the work I longed to do. I'd grown up seeing again and again how women's voices were missing from the world, and now I was seeing the inner side of that dynamic—what caused women, including myself, to hold back our ideas and our voices.

A couple of years into juggling part-time coaching with full-time employment, I decided to leave the foundation. My blog, which had begun with thirty-eight friends and family subscribers, had grown to a readership of a few thousand women. I started to think about bringing the coaching work I did to the larger audience of these readers, and I wanted to know what kinds of workshops or courses would be most useful to them. So in a survey, I asked them, "What's the biggest challenge in your life?"

I offered a big multiple-choice list of answers, a list of the challenges we typically talk about as looming large in contemporary women's lives: work-life balance, stress, not enough time, financial problems, health challenges, relationship issues. But then, because of what I'd seen in my clients, my friends, and myself, I added one more challenge to the list: "I'm playing small."

When the survey responses came back, "I'm playing small" was what the largest number of women deemed their most significant problem—yes, more than work-life balance, stress, or relationship issues. There was indeed a larger phenomenon reflective of what I was observing: Bright, full-of-potential women were playing small, and they were *aware* of this and they didn't like it. In fact, many saw playing small as the most pressing challenge in their lives.

In some sense, what I'm now doing is the very same thing I did that day in high school when I decided to try to change the English curriculum. I'm working to bring forward women's voices where they are absent, because I believe those voices will help us create a better world.

On Doing Inner Work

A year ago, I was appearing as a guest on a live morning news show. Fewer than ten minutes before my airtime, the producer of my segment walked in. "Here's the introduction the anchors will be using for you," she said. She showed me a bright purple piece of paper with a script that said, "Recent studies show that even though women account for 51 percent of middle managers in the US, they are only 4 percent of Fortune 500 CEOs. Our next guest says there's no one to blame but ourselves. . . . She says women tend to do things that undermine us and our work. Welcome, Tara Sophia Mohr!"

Uh-oh.

In any moment of the day, I would not have looked forward to standing up to the producer, and I especially wasn't in the mood for it in my early-morning, pre-TV nervous and exhausted state. But I heard myself think, I'm not going down like that.

I figured this was a *news* show, so I'd try an accuracy angle. "Oh, you'll want to change that because it's inaccurate," I said casually. "I'd never say that women have no one to blame but themselves for those statistics, because many external factors—like discrimination—lead to those numbers."

"Oh, okay . . . ," she said reluctantly. "I can ask the executive producer about changing it, but it's doubtful . . ."

I could tell that if I wanted this to get changed in the next ten minutes, I needed to supply an easy solution. "How about if we change it to 'Our next guest, Tara Sophia Mohr, says women can do something to change those numbers'?" I asked her.

"Hmmm, I'll check," she said.

They changed the introduction.

The script the producer originally showed me perfectly reflected our collective confusion about the question of "external" versus "internal" barriers to women's career advancement. Our usual cultural conversation divides the challenges into two categories: unfair external barriers to women's advancement that women are victims of (discrimination, bias, poor work-family policies, pay disparities) and internal, psychological things that women "do to themselves" and for which women are therefore to blame. A rather ridiculous debate follows: "Are the internal or external barriers more important? Is this all women's responsibility or is it not 'their fault'?" The producers' assumption was that if we were talking about what women do to undermine themselves, "it's women's fault." It was "their choice."

I see it differently. Centuries of women's exclusion from political, public, and professional life have had many effects. Some of those effects were *external*: legislation, formal policies, pay disparities, lack of legal protections, and the denial of women's basic rights. But inequality of men and women has also left *internal effects* in us. Over generations, it shaped how we think of ourselves and what we see as possible for our lives and work. It shaped our fears—fears of speaking up, of rocking the boat, of displeasing others. It caused women to develop a number of behaviors that enabled them to survive in environments where they had no legal, financial, or political power—behaviors like conflict avoidance, self-censoring, people-pleasing, tentative speech and action.

While we've done a great deal of work collectively, especially over the past forty years, to remove the external barriers to women's empowerment, we have not taken the same close look at the internal legacy of inequality and how to change it. We have a lot of inner unlearning and relearning to do.

The tools you'll acquire in this book are for playing bigger in the ways you most want to; but at a deeper level, they are tools for unlearning the lessons that centuries of women's marginalization have left in each of us.

About the Book

People often ask me, "Where does the Playing Big material you teach come from?" It's a hybrid. Some comes from my business school training. Some comes from twenty years of learning about psychology and personal growth. Some comes from the wisdom of the spiritual texts I grew up reading. Some comes from the lessons I've learned on my personal journey. And of course, much comes from what I learned working with women to help them play bigger.

What often felt like a disjointed split in my childhood between heart and mind, intuition and education, right brain and left brain, has become a unique blend that I bring to my work. There's the MBA in me and the spiritual seeker. The part of me that loves intellectual rigor and the part that loves poetry. So in these pages, you'll learn tools as tactical as research-based communication techniques and as soulful as a two-thousand-year-old spiritual teaching about fear. I teach both because both can help you play bigger.

We'll begin by talking about what most fundamentally gets in the way of women playing big. It's the voice of self-doubt, of "not me"—the voice inside that is sure you aren't the one to lead, to write the book, to take on that bigger role, to speak up in the meeting. It's the voice that tells you that you aren't qualified enough, smart enough, experienced enough, good-at-*x*-enough . . . to ever play big. I know you are familiar with this voice, and you probably have some sense of how self-doubt has held you back in your work or in your personal life. In chapter 1, you'll learn what to do when you feel insecure or self-critical, so that all those thoughts no longer get in your way. I *love* teaching women this because it's actually relatively easy to change how we relate to self-doubt—once you have the right understanding of your inner critic and the appropriate tools to use the moment it acts up.

Once you're not listening so much to your inner critic, you have the opportunity to listen to a very different voice within. After working with thousands of women to help them play bigger, I know this: *Every* woman has at her core unfailing, perfect wisdom. When you have a dilemma, the wise part of you knows what next step is right. When you are feeling confused, the wise part of you has clarity. When a problem seems overwhelming and complicated, the wise part of you has a simple, elegant answer. I call this core your inner mentor, because it's like having an advisor and supporter inside your own mind—and therefore available to you around the clock. In chapter 2, you'll learn how you can access and start taking direction from this part of yourself.

Learning how to listen to your inner mentor instead of your inner critic is the first major movement toward playing bigger. Playing big doesn't come from working more, pushing harder, or finding confidence. It comes from listening to the most powerful and secure part of you, not the voice of self-doubt.

Then we tackle the other obstacles that most commonly hold women back from playing bigger. First: fear. Whether it's fear of failure, of standing out from the crowd, of conflict, or of greater visibility, fears hold back most women from sharing their voices and ideas. And yet, not all fear is problematic. In chapter 3, we'll cover two types of fear. One kind of fear keeps us playing small; one kind is an essential ingredient for playing big. The task before us is to shift out of that limiting type of fear and welcome the positive kind. You'll learn how to distinguish between the two and what to do when each one arises.

Next we turn to unhooking from praise and criticism. Attachment to praise and avoidance of criticism keeps us from doing innovative, controversial work and—more simply—from following the paths we feel called toward, whether or not those around us understand or approve. And powerful women are often met with hostile criticism, so we need to learn how to receive it and not be paralyzed by it. We also need to learn to interpret feedback so that it propels us forward rather than hurting or immobilizing us.

Then we look at what we've all learned in school and how it can stand in the way of our playing big. I started to notice a surprising phenomenon in my work with women. I expected that women who excelled in school would also excel in their careers. After all, wasn't school—particularly college and graduate school—preparation for the work world? Yet again and again I saw that women who were stars in school ran into major, self-imposed walls in their careers. As I dug deeper, I understood that they were struggling because school cultivates and rewards a particular way of working that not only doesn't help us play bigger but often *gets in the way* of our playing bigger. Chapter 5 is about how to leave behind the good-student habits we are conditioned in for our many years in school and that we need to unlearn in our adult lives.

In the second half of the book, we move into talking about action. I share some of the most common ways we stall on playing big and hide our brilliance. Typically, when women read about these hiding strategies, they have a few "uh-oh" moments as they come to recognize how they've been unconsciously putting their playing big on hold. Once you see which ones you are using, you can't go back to them in the same way anymore; you've brought them into the light of awareness.

The antidote to all that hiding and stalling is a special kind of action called a leap. A leap is an immediate, experimental, simple act—the exact opposite of the overplanned, overthought, perfectionist action so many brilliant women are most comfortable taking. A leap stretches you into playing much bigger, *right now.*

Then we turn to how we present ourselves through our communication. Whenever I teach about the subtle ways we undermine ourselves with our words, I receive a huge response from women saying, "Wow, I didn't realize those things were making me come across less powerfully, but now I see it!" It's incredibly powerful to change undermining communication habits so that you are perceived as the intelligent and strong woman you are, and it can even be fun to work on them, especially with a friend or colleague. Chapter 8 is about shifting from speech and writing that diminishes you to communication that conveys confidence, competence, and warmth.

Next we talk about callings. Each of us is gifted with callings. A calling is the pull you feel to address a particular need in the world. For example, you might feel a calling to run for city council, teach yoga to teens, or volunteer to support veterans in your town. You might feel a calling to a certain career change or to launch a new initiative in your company. We all have callings, but most of the time we play small by denying them. One of the most important and fulfilling parts of playing bigger is moving from resisting your callings to embracing them.

In the last chapter, I discuss how to *sustain* playing big. We've all had the experience of pursuing a goal with gusto for a while, thinking self-discipline will be enough to help us achieve it, but then finding that motivation fades. We end up disappointed in ourselves and not taking action. This chapter explores a very different way of maintaining motivation and achieving big results, one that's based on self-care.

And finally, in the conclusion, we'll talk about the big picture, the journey ahead, and what is for me the most important shift we make when we move from playing small to playing big: to not just succeed within systems as they are but transform them to be better—more humane, just, safe, and supportive for human beings.

At the end of each chapter, you'll have the opportunity to apply the ideas to your own life and put them into practice through exercises and journaling questions. I know you are busy, so the exercises never take more than a few minutes, and in most cases, they don't take extra time at all; they'll just give you a new way of thinking about and approaching the challenges that cross your path.

Journaling is a tool for playing bigger because change begins with self-awareness. Writing enables you to figure out what you are *really* thinking and *really* feeling. While we can often get into unhelpful rumination or worrying when we simply ponder a topic, when we write about it we move forward in our thinking. New truths emerge after three or five or ten minutes of putting pen to paper.

This book is for brilliant women like you. I wrote it so that you can move forward in pursuing whatever calls to you, so that your greatest gifts find expression. I wrote it because I'm tired of meeting women who have important messages to share but whose self-doubt is keeping them quiet. I'm tired of encountering woman after woman deluded by the myth that she needs to be more something—more qualified, more prepared, more expert—than she is in order to share her ideas. I wrote it out of allegiance to the art not yet made, the companies not yet founded, the books and op-ed columns not yet written, the critiques not yet voiced. I wrote it because all those expressions of goodness, of insight, of beauty, hang in the balance. I wrote this book because I want our world to be changed by you.

PLAYING BIG

CHAPTER I

• • •

The Inner Critic

I recently had lunch with a colleague—an executive coach and business consultant. She's worked at the most prestigious consulting companies and maintains a roster of executive clients who find her advice indispensible. Over our meal, she explained to me that she wanted to do more public speaking, sharing the ideas she'd developed in her consulting practice with a much wider audience. She sounded eager and ready to go, uncertain only about what practical steps to take next.

I offered to introduce her to a few speaking agents who I thought would love to work with her and could help her secure engagements. Suddenly, she started talking about how she needed to spend some months doing small, local talks to "hone her craft." A new narrative came out, about how she wasn't really ready to take her speaking to a large stage. Having just watched a video of her giving a speech, I knew this wasn't the case.

I was hearing in her something I've now heard in hundreds of women. I think of it as "the voice of not-me"—the internal chatter that tells a woman she's not ready to lead, she's not enough of an expert, she's not good enough at this or that. It's the voice of self-doubt, of the inner critic. We begin our journey here because it is what most holds women back from playing bigger.

All women grapple with this voice of self-doubt in one way or another. For some women, it is most prominent around their professional lives. For others, it comes up around their sense of competence as mothers or partners. For others, it speaks mostly about appearance, body image, or aging. And for others, it chatters most loudly about their creative dreams—to make music or paint or write. We are so used to living with this voice, most of us don't imagine it could be otherwise. It's become the background noise we live with. Since women don't talk to one another about the most vicious things it says, we don't hear counterarguments or get support, and we don't learn that other women—women we admire because they seem so confident—hear the same irrational, harsh voice in their heads too.

The costs of women's self-doubt are enormous. Think of all the ideas unshared, businesses not started, important questions not raised, talents unused. Think of all the fulfillment and joy not experienced because self-doubt keeps us from going for the opportunities that would bring that joy and fulfillment. This is the bad news around women's self-doubt: how pervasive it is, and how much has been lost because of it.

Yet there is also good news about women's self-doubt—and the good news is less well-known: While "confidence issues" *seem* complex and difficult to address, they don't need to be. It turns out you don't have to find a magic source of confidence, dig deep into childhood wounds to find the roots of your insecurities, or figure out how to permanently banish that critical voice in your head. Instead, *you simply need to learn how to live with the inner voice of self-doubt but not be held back by it, to hear the voice and not take direction from it*. Best news of all? You can learn to do that quickly, with simple tools you'll learn in this chapter.

Because self-doubt is so destructive when not dealt with, yet so manageable once you know those tools, I've become passionate about every woman and girl on the planet receiving what I think of as Inner Critic 101 Training. You'll receive that training in the pages that follow. I've come to believe that knowing how to work effectively with your own self-doubt is a basic and necessary life skill, an even more basic and necessary life skill than driving or cooking yourself a meal. Imagine what a different world we'd live in if every girl learned what the voice of her inner critic sounded like and what to do to quiet it, if she were unhampered by self-doubt as she moved through her turbulent teen years and into adulthood. Imagine the different course your life would have taken had you been taught the what and why of that critical voice inside and learned some techniques to use so that it didn't get in your way. In this chapter, you'll get that training, for yourself and so you can pass it on to others. Most important, you'll learn what you can do moment to moment so that self-doubt no longer stands in the way of your playing big.

What Is the Inner Critic?

When I talk about the inner critic or the voice of "not-me," I'm speaking about the voice in our heads characterized by the eleven qualities that follow. You probably won't notice all eleven qualities in everything your voice of self-doubt says, but you'll usually notice at least a few of these qualities when they speak.

1. **Harsh, rude, mean.** When you hear a voice in your head saying harsh things to you that you would never intend to say to a person you love, you're hearing the inner critic.

2. **Binary.** The inner critic is a black-and-white thinker. You are awesome or you are pathetic. You are gorgeous or ugly. You are a fabulous friend or a horrible one. Your dreams are possible or they aren't. When the inner critic speaks, there's usually no room for gray.

3. **Ostensibly, the voice of reason.** This voice argues for what seems to be in your best interest, what is realistic and effective. For example, "If you go forward with the book, you'll ruin your reputation. Your work isn't ready for that level of scrutiny. Better to hold off for a while." Or "You are much better off studying someone else's theories and approach to this kind of consulting work before you pitch potential clients. People won't take you seriously unless you are steeped in a well-known method. Your own ideas aren't enough."

4. **The voice of "You aren't ready yet."** For women, this voice often manifests as "You aren't ready yet." "You need another degree." "You need more time to prepare." "You need more experience."

5. **The voice of "You aren't good at math/negotiating/technical stuff."** For many women, the voice of self-doubt shows up most strongly around those skills and activities that are associated with masculinity in our culture and, unconsciously, often in our own minds. This includes quantitative skills, negotiation, technical tasks, financial matters, and—unfortunately—sometimes leadership more broadly.

6. **The voice of body-perfectionism.** Another common expression of this voice is self-critical thoughts around body, weight, appearance, or aging. "You aren't attractive anymore." "Oh my God, look at your upper arms." "You look fat in this." "You need to lose ten pounds, by yesterday."

7. **The tape.** The inner critic's voice often feels like an audio tape that's running automatically in your head, rather than like thoughts you consciously author and generate. It may even feel as if the critic tape invades and interrupts your own thinking.

8. **A broken record.** The inner critic will come up with new lines from time to time, but it also tends to rehash a few core narratives it has been repeating to you for decades.

9. **Irrational but persistent.** Often we *know* that what the fearful voice in our heads says is irrational, yet it still has power over us.

10. **The one-two punch.** The one-two punch goes like this. Let's say first, the inner critic starts mumbling to you about how everyone else in the room has it more together than you do. Then the critic follows up with "Get a grip, get some perspective." Or "What is wrong with you? *Other people* are confident and relaxed . . . just look over there, at Susan. . . ." In other words, the critic first attacks you with critical thoughts, and then shames you for having those thoughts. That is its one-two punch.

11. **The inner critic may take inspiration from critical people in your life.** You may hear echoes of a critical parent, a sibling, or a boss in your inner critic's voice. Or you may hear echoes of the ethos of major cultural

forces such as your religion, company, or country. Our outer critics come to exist inside our own heads.

The Inner Critic versus Realistic Thinking

Often women say to me, "But there are things I'm truly not qualified for, or not good at. How do I know if I'm hearing my inner critic talking or if I'm just being realistic?" That's a really important question, because, of course, there are things we aren't ready for and we all have weaknesses in our abilities. In addition to using the list of the eleven qualities of the inner critic's voice, here's how you can tell the difference between the irrational inner critic and solid realistic thinking.

Inner Critic	Realistic Thinking
Makes definite pronouncements about the situation	Asks curious questions about the situation
Has no interest in actual evidence	Interested in gathering evidence to inform conclusions
Thinks and speaks in black-and-white terms	Is able to deal with complexity and gray areas
Asks binary yes/no questions ("Is it possible? Yes or no? Am I qualified? Yes or no?")	Asks helpful, open-ended questions ("How might it be possible? What part of this looks possible?")
Is repetitive	Is forward-moving
Focuses on problems/areas of lack	Seeks solutions
Speaks in an anxious tone	Speaks in a calmer tone
Speaks from a fundamental stance of self-critique	Speaks from a fundamental stance of self-support

The realistic thinker in us is forward-moving. She seeks solutions. The critic will spin and spin, ruminating on the risks and worst-case scenarios. The critic often speaks in an anxious, emotionally charged tone. The realistic thinker is grounded, clear-eyed, calm. Many of us hold the belief that "realistic thinking" is skeptical if not pessimistic, but in fact *realistic thinking is inquisitive, exploratory, and highly creative.*

For two decades, Claire worked in retail companies, always wanting to start one of her own. When she contemplated that dream, she heard a stream of thoughts that sounded like this:

> "I would love to start a retail business. I would love the independence and challenge. I feel like it's what I am meant to do . . . but I don't have what that takes. I need much more experience; I don't have the access to capital, and doing this would be irresponsible to my family. I would be putting them at great financial risk."

How do we know whether this is her inner critic talking, or if she's engaging in good, realistic thinking? We can recognize the inner critic in Claire by a couple of clues:

- It's making **definite pronouncements about what's true**: "I don't have what it takes." There's no evidence gathering or real exploration. There are no open-ended or curious questions about the truth of the situation.
- There's an **escalation of worry**: "I need a broader skill set . . ." quickly escalates to "I'd be putting my family at great financial risk." Worst-case-scenario thinking is a hallmark quality of the inner critic.

- It's especially concerned about those aspects of the work that are traditionally **associated with masculinity**: raising capital and earning money to support one's family.

Here's how "realistic thinking" on the same topic might go:

> "I would love to start a retail business. I feel like it's what I am meant to do. . . . I don't know if I have what is needed. I wonder how I could find out and see how that fits with where I am. I'll do x to learn more about that this week . . . that feels exciting, and a little scary too. And, of course, I'm really committed to supporting my family financially. I wonder how I can do this and maintain support for them."

You can hear the different tone in the second example: more positive, supportive, exploratory, and in fact much more rational. There is an interest in real information gathering. There is a focus on the topic itself, not on ego distractions about measuring up or not.

Why Do We Have Inner Critics?

Why do we have this self-critical voice inside? Is it because of tough childhoods, our patriarchal culture, our stressful modern lives?

We don't need to have had particular life experiences to develop a harsh inner critic. We're hardwired for it. The inner critic is an expression of the safety instinct in us—the part of us that wants to stay safe from potential emotional risk—from hurt, failure, criticism, disappointment, or rejection by the tribe. The safety instinct is cunning. If it simply said to you, "No, don't compose the song, don't run for office, don't make the career change, don't share your ideas—it's too risky," you wouldn't listen. You'd probably reply something along the lines of "No, I feel okay about the risks. Here I go." So the safety instinct uses a more effective argument: "Your paintings are terrible." "Your book won't offer anything new—there are so many books on the subject." "Your attempt at career change will cause you to end up broke." The inner critic speaks up with more viciousness and volume when we are exposing ourselves to a real or perceived vulnerability—something that triggers a fear of embarrassment, rejection, failure, or pain.

Playing big—following our callings and dreams—puts us all in a vulnerable place, but for women the stakes are especially high. We know playing bigger may bring painful criticism or rejection, that others may call us "uppity," not likable, too aggressive, bitchy, angry, not nice. We've watched that happen time and time again to women on the national stage. We've read violent, objectifying, often vulgar comments made about prominent women—particularly in online media. Our own safety instinct seeks to protect us from that external criticism by spewing cruel self-criticisms ("You aren't ready for that, you don't know what you are talking about") that keep us from stretching into greater visibility and encountering those kinds of attacks.

It's as if you've got internal departments and the inner critic works for the Risk Aversion Department. The folks over at the Risk Aversion Department don't coordinate with the folks in the Fulfillment Department. They don't care if you have a fulfilled or self-actualized day in your life! They'll be pleased if you feel relatively bored, numbed out, and sad—as long as you stay stuck in the zone of the familiar.

For this reason, the folks at Risk Aversion don't worry about whether what they say to you is true or not. This is the big "aha" that we all need to have around our self-doubt. What the inner critic says—"You aren't ready. You don't know what you are talking about. That idea/question/creation has no value"—just isn't true. Being accurate isn't the aim of the inner critic; getting you to avoid emotional risk is. When we understand that our safety instinct uses the inner critic as a strategy, and that its chatter is not a reflection of reality, we take away its power. We can say to ourselves in the moment, "I hear that voice, but I *know* it's not the voice of truth, and I choose not to take direction from it."

You'll Hear Self-Doubt Most Loudly When . . .

Many women find their inner critic speaks up most loudly around their most deeply felt dreams for their lives and work, because we feel particularly vulnerable about them. They experience the most panicky, overwhelming self-doubt when they are moving toward what they truly long to do. The inner critic is like a guard at the edge of your comfort zone. As long as you don't venture forth out of that zone, the inner critic can leave you alone—like a guard taking a nap. Yet when you approach the edge of your comfort zone, test old beliefs, contemplate change, or stretch into playing bigger, you wake the sleeping guard. The inner critic recites its lines in an attempt to get you to go back into the familiar zone of the status quo. Many women find that the more strongly the inner critic shows up, the louder and meaner and more hysterical its voice, the closer they are to a breakthrough or the more likely they are to be on the edge of taking a very important step. In this sense, when you hear a major inner critic attack, you can often greet it as good news: It likely means you are playing bigger.

We can get confused if we've been taught that we'll feel good or excited when we're on the right track. In fact, often when we start doing what we most want to do in our professional lives—or when we even contemplate doing so—we actually feel a sense of discomfort. Many women mistakenly think all those doubts and uncomfortable feelings mean they aren't on the right path after all. But really, we've just woken the sleeping guard at the edge of the comfort zone.

But What If My Inner Critic Motivates Me?

Now that you have a sense of what the inner critic is, we'll turn to the tools and practices you can use, moment to moment, to lessen its influence in your life. But first, there's one concern women often bring up when I teach about this topic that I want to address. It's a concern that I could never have predicted: Many women aren't sure they *want* to quiet their inner critics! After all, they ask me, isn't the inner critic part of what motivates us to do meticulous, excellent work?

I first heard this question a few years ago, when I taught a workshop about the inner critic at a major accounting firm. A woman in the front row raised her hand. "I hear what you are saying about how the inner critic holds us back, but honestly, if I stopped listening to my inner critic, I'd be a total slacker. My inner critic is what motivates me to work hard and perform. Can't the inner critic be a positive force?"

As is true for so many of us, her inner critic was a kind of a companion with whom she had a tried-and-true partnership: The critic hurled words of panic and disparagement, and she ran on the treadmill harder, producing careful, thorough work. This cycle—

played out dozens of times each day—had produced some really good professional results.

This was my response to her, and it's my response to you if you share her question: Self-doubt *can* indeed motivate us to work hard and achieve, but there are *serious costs* to being motivated this way.

- **Costs to your quality of life.** How much joy can you experience in your work if fear and a soundtrack of harsh thoughts about yourself play in your head every day?

- **Costs to your professional life.** The critic can lead us to work hard, but it often leads us to do the *wrong* work. When motivated by the critic, we'll dot all the *i*'s and cross all the *t*'s (many times over), but the inner critic can't motivate us to take the intelligent risks—doing stretch assignments, speaking up, developing key relationships—that dramatically advance our careers. *The inner critic can motivate you to be a meticulous worker bee, but it can't motivate you to be a game changer.*

- **Playing bigger costs.** Whatever playing big looks like for you, think about this: Can your inner critic really help you do that more boldly, more quickly, and with greater enjoyment? Can your inner critic motivate you to pursue your callings? No.

- **Health costs.** When we are motivated by fear of failure, stress hormones flood our systems. Long-term stress is correlated with a variety of health problems, from heart disease to asthma to depression. Human bodies are not designed to be in a stressed state for hours each day, and it wrecks our health if we are.

If you care about your physical, emotional, and spiritual well-being, listening to the inner critic is not a viable way to stay motivated.

In some sense, the woman at the accounting firm who asked the question was correct: If she let go of her inner critic, she might, indeed, have trouble getting motivated for a while. But in that fallow time, she'd have the space to begin to discover where her natural river of motivation lay. She'd either find a *positive* reason to get excited about performing with excellence in her current job, such as doing incredible work with her team, sharing her talents in the world, and earning more for her family, or she'd need to explore alternative roles that sparked more of her passion.

Noticing and Naming the Critic

Now let's turn to what you can do day to day, moment to moment, self-doubting thought to self-doubting thought, to quiet your inner critic.

The day of unfailing, gorgeous confidence isn't coming. Self-doubt will always be a part of what we each work with as we take steps to play bigger. The name of the game is not eliminating self-doubt. *The name of the game is learning how to let the inner critic do its thing, without taking direction from it. The goal is to hear the inner critic's voice but not let that voice determine your choices.*

Bestselling author Dani Shapiro's work has appeared in *The New Yorker, Elle, The New York Times Book Review,* and the *Los Angeles Times.* She has taught in the writing programs at Columbia University and NYU. By any account, she has plenty of evidence that she's a successful writer. And yet here's what she has to say about self-doubt showing up in her writing process:

"I was looking at my computer one day at my list of everything I had written in the last few years—essays, stories, books, blog posts, everything. I realized that every single one of these pieces had begun with the words running through my mind, 'Here goes nothing. Here goes nothing. It's not going to work this time. . . . I know it's worked before, but this time somehow I'm in over my head. I'm not going to get it right, I'm not going to be able to figure it out. But you know what? I'm gonna do it anyway.' . . . I've had this practice for so many years now, of hearing that voice say, 'You can't do this,' and not listening to that voice. We all have that voice, I call it our inner sensor. It's always sitting on our shoulder in some way and it says different things to each of us. It says, 'You're stupid,' or, 'Someone else did it better,' or, 'How dare you? What right do you have?' . . . **The practice is in quieting that voice, not banishing it.**"

Cherry Murray is the dean of the Harvard School of Engineering and Applied Sciences. Prior to her tenure at Harvard, she led some of the nation's most brilliant scientists and engineers as an executive at Bell Laboratories and the Lawrence Livermore National Laboratory. As described in an article in *Nature*, "She has published more than 70 papers in peer-reviewed journals, has won a number of awards, holds two patents and has served on more than 80 national and international scientific committees and governing boards. Yet the self-doubt still lurks. 'Do I ever think I'm not qualified?' she says. 'All the time.'"

Twyla Tharp, award-winning choreographer, describes in *The Creative Habit* the five big fears that still play out in her artistic life:

"1. People will laugh at me. 2. Someone has done it before. 3. I have nothing to say. 4. I will upset someone I love. 5. Once executed, the idea will never be as good as it is in my mind."

She writes, "If I let them, they'll shut down my impulses ('No, you can't do that') and perhaps turn off the spigots of creativity altogether."

I think of it this way: If women like these, women at the very top of their fields who have every reason to feel confident, continue to grapple with regular and serious self-doubt, you and I probably will too. In fact, these women grapple with self-doubt *because* they are playing big, regularly exposing themselves to criticism and visible failures and expressing their unique ideas and leadership in the world. Their words show that they've been able to play big because they know to recognize the inner critic as just *a* voice within—not the ultimate authority.

It almost seems too easy, but it's true: You don't have to do all that much with your inner critic. In a culture that is all about doing, this is a counterintuitive truth. Recognizing the critic's voice consciously is often enough to immediately snap us out of its trance.

Why is noticing and naming the voice of self-doubt so powerful? Liberating yourself from the influence of the inner critic depends on a very simple insight. You are not the critical voice. You are the person *aware* of the critical voice. You are the person feeling perplexed by it or bummed out by it or believing it. You are the person trying to understand it and work with it and get rid of it. You are the entity that is hearing the voice. The critic is not the core of you. The core of you is the you of your aspirations, of your inner wisdom. The critic is a kind of intruder. It's a voice that happens to play in your mind, but it is not who you really are.

Most of us are untrained in differentiating the various voices we hear in our thoughts. We think they are all "us" in the same way. As you name the inner critic voice when it shows up, you begin to unbraid it from the other strands of "you": your imagination, your aspirations, your wisdom. By saying, "Oh, I'm hearing the critic right now," you can remember that's all it is and move forward despite its rants and threats.

But What If the Critical Voice Really Is Me?

Many times, when I introduce the idea that the critic is not who we really are, a woman in the room will say to me, "No, Tara, this *is* who I really am. This is how my voice, my thinking sounds. This is the 'me' I know in my own head." A few others will nod as they listen to her. If you feel that way, it simply means the critic has taken over—temporarily—as the dominant voice within. This can happen for a number of reasons:

- **Working in a role or attending an academic program in which critical thinking is the dominant mode.** When we spend years strengthening the critical-thinking muscle (poking holes in ideas, finding the problems with potential solutions, etc.), assessment, skepticism, and criticism become the dominant modes with which we respond not only to our work but also to our own burgeoning dreams. When it comes to our aspirations, a more nurturing and generative response would serve us better.

- **We received consistent criticism from key people in our lives in early childhood** and have internalized their voices.

- **The critic has won out—for now.** For many women, there is a self-compounding quality to the inner critic. Once allowed to be in charge, the critic takes more and more control, as if a conqueror gathering territory. Like an untreated, progressive disease, this worsens over time. As it does, your comfort zone shrinks and ossifies. When that happens, you will start to feel like the inner critic is "just you" because it's the primary voice in your head.

If you feel like the inner critic is "just who you are," rest assured: It's not. You are in for some wonderful, liberating changes as you use the practices in this chapter. You'll start to hear and know the other voices within. I promise.

The Practices: What to Do, Moment to Moment, When Self-Doubt Shows Up

1. **Label and notice.** When you hear your critic talking, label this voice by simply saying to yourself, "Oh, I'm hearing my inner critic right now." This is the foundational inner critic practice on which all the others depend.

2. **Separate the "I" from the inner critic.** For example, you might say, "*My inner critic* is having a little freak-out right now" rather than "*I'm* having a freak-out right now." When you refer to the inner critic as the inner critic, instead of conflating it with the core "I" of you,

you train your mind that the critic is simply one voice within you and not the primary one.

3. **Create a character that personifies your inner critic.** This is a great tool that I learned from the Coaches Training Institute. The journaling questions and examples later in this chapter will guide you, step by step, in doing this. When you create a character with a name and visual image, you help yourself remember that the critic is not the core of you, it's one voice, with its own personality and pathology. It's easier to get a handle on the critic because you can see its words as coming from a finite (and usually rather absurd) character. You can begin to have a sense of humor about the critic too. After all, what it's saying is usually ridiculous!

4. **Compassionately see your inner critic's motives.** When you hear the critic, check in and ask that voice of self-doubt, "What are you trying to do right now? What harm are you trying to protect me from?" Once you've created an inner critic character, you can picture your character and actually ask him or her, in your mind's eye, what his or her motivation is. You might ask what he or she is most afraid of. Once you are in touch with the root of the critic's intentions, respond with compassion toward the critic's misguided attempt to keep you safe—usually from attack, embarrassment, isolation, or failure. A great way to do this is to acknowledge those motives and then sincerely respond with, "Thanks so much for your input, but I've got this one covered."

5. **Look for the humor.** Ask yourself, What is absurd or funny about what my critic is saying right now?

6. **Remove your critic from the scene.** Either stand up and "act out" walking your inner critic character into a different space or imagine him or her going off to a different place. Then begin your work again knowing "It's just me here—the inner critic is on a break for now."

7. **Pantomime putting all your inner critic thoughts into a vessel (a cup, bowl, box).** Then move that vessel out of the room and begin your work again with the sense that the critic isn't present in the room with you anymore.

8. **Picture the voice receding into space.** Notice where, physically, it feels like the inner critic voice is located in or around your body, and picture the voice receding into space, moving away from you.

9. **Imagine you can simply turn down the volume on the critic's voice.** See an "inner critic volume dial" in your mind's eye and turn the volume way down.

Inner Critic Don'ts: Arguing and Attacks

These nine tools give you lots of options for what to do when the inner critic shows up. There are also a couple important "don'ts"—what *not* to do when you hear the critic.

Fitness coach Jillian Michaels is known as "America's Toughest Trainer." A couple of years ago, we talked about the inner critic on her radio show, and we explored how Jillian's inner critic had impacted her.

Jillian asked me what we do after we acknowledge the critic: "Tell her to piss off?" she asked. She was starting to see all the ways her critic had held her back, and understandably, she was getting angry about it.

"Well, how well has that worked in the past?" I asked Jillian.

"Well, she's not gone . . . ," she answered.

Jillian had the instinct many of us have: to make the inner critic the enemy and blast it with anger. That can feel like an empowered response, but it's not. We don't ever want to make a part of us the enemy, to go to war with a part of ourselves. Plus, an angry, forceful response doesn't make the inner critic shrink away. In fact, it can strengthen the critic's power.

Why? Imagine for a moment that the inner critic voice is a very afraid child misbehaving because of his or her terror. Would telling that child to "leave you alone" or "shut up" cause the child to behave better? No. Reassurance, love, and addressing the child's underlying fears would. The critic is like that child, stemming from a very afraid part of ourselves. By getting angry at it, we often just inflame it.

Jillian and I talked about how else one could respond: noticing and naming the critic, understanding the critic's motivations of self-protection so that we could then reassure the afraid part of ourselves and move forward in spite of the critic's doubts.

Like getting angry, *arguing with the voice of self-doubt* is another knee-jerk response many of us have, and it's just as ineffective as a forceful or angry response. Arguing sounds like this:

Your critic says: "You look ugly!"
You say (or try to say) back, "No, I look great in this!"
Your critic says, "You aren't prepared enough for this presentation—you are about to lose this client!"
You say, "No, I won't—I did a good job preparing!"

We never win arguments with our inner critics. When you spend any time arguing with the critic, the critic is "winning" because while you are busy arguing with it, you are not doing your thing, putting your voice out there, risking failure to fulfill your aspirations, nurturing your budding dreams. Plus, your critic has a long list of reasons you shouldn't play bigger, and if you successfully win the argument about reason #84, the critic will simply move on to reason #85. It's a rabbit hole. *You don't have to win the argument with your inner critic; you have to step away from the conversation.*

You can do this with the simple "Oh, I'm hearing the critic now" that we've talked about—by noticing and naming the critic's voice. You can also add a second tool from the list: investigating the critic's motives. When you hear the voice of self-doubt, ask that voice, "What are you trying to do? What are you trying to prevent or protect me from?" When you are in touch with its underlying motives, you can compassionately see the inner critic's intentions: to keep you safe from the kinds of attack, embarrassment, or isolation it most fears.

My own inner critic often comes up when I head into certain speaking engagements ("This audience will never go for this! You don't have enough research backing up what you are going to say!") or when I have a media appearance coming up ("You haven't been taking good care of yourself and you're going to look horrible. You didn't go over your talking points. You are totally unprepared for this one!").

One of my favorite things to say back to my own inner critic in these situations is this simple sentence: **"Thanks, but I've got this one covered."** That "thank you" is sincere, not flippant. When I say it, I feel real appreciation for the critic's attempt to protect me from potential embarrassment or failure in these highly visible moments. In the "but I've got this one covered," the more mature me takes back the steering wheel, reassuring the fearful part of me that things are okay. It's like finding the calm, responsible adult within who can say to the hysterical child, "You don't need to worry. I'll take care of us here." When I say those words, I'm neither arguing with the critic nor repressing it. I'm hearing the objection, providing some reassurance, and moving on.

What If My Inner Critic Character Is My Mom?

A few years ago, I gave a workshop on the inner critic for a large national women's organization. Most of the women in the audience were over sixty and had been pioneers—among the first women in their professional fields.

How would they respond to the topic of the inner critic, I wondered. Would they still be grappling with the voice of self-doubt, or would they have moved far beyond it? Or would women who had been such trailblazers have been relatively free from self-doubt all along?

As I spoke about the inner critic, there was lots of nodding, laughter, and tears of recognition. One woman in the back raised her hand. "My inner critic voice is my mother's internalized voice," she said, "and I'm wondering how many other women in the room that was true for too."

We did a show of hands. About three-quarters of the hands in the room went up. Three-quarters of the women in the room had seen some version of their mothers as their inner critic.

This was new. When I teach an inner critic workshop to mid-career or early-career women, usually some notice that their inner critic connects to their mother's voice, but that connection is not nearly as common as it was for these older women.

I told the women in the room that the prevalence of mother

inner critics was unusual and asked them what they thought about it. "Our mothers raised us in a very different time. They were teaching us how to be appropriate women—the kind of women who could survive in the culture. We were taught to be polite, to find a good husband, to take care of our children—to focus on family first." I wonder if this is an expression of the progress women have made. Liberated themselves, perhaps far fewer mothers today are imparting the kinds of beliefs and judgments that become a harsh inner critic voice inside their daughters.

But no matter what your age, you aren't alone if you've noticed that your inner critic is an echo of your mother's voice. After all, no one has as formative an impact on our psyches as our mothers. But you also aren't alone if you notice your inner critic voice is an echo of your father's voice, or your sisters', or your brothers'. None of those are uncommon either.

Or perhaps you notice the voice of a significant mentor, professor, or boss. On another occasion, I gave an inner critic workshop to women in a large law firm. There were about fifty partners, junior partners, and associates in the room.

People had seemed engaged and were taking lots of notes, but when I asked people to write down a description of a character who personified their critic, and to give that character a name, the room went totally silent. I looked around and saw that all the pens in the room stopped moving. I assumed I hadn't given clear directions for the writing exercise, so I repeated them, this time paying more attention to my words. Still, no pens moved.

"I'm noticing no one is writing," I said, a little nervously. My own inner critic was getting worried that the material was too out-there for them and they had given up on me. "Did the instructions make sense?"

"Oh, yes, they made sense," one of the younger women in the room said, with a kind of chuckle in her voice. "I just can't write this stuff down about my inner critic character because it's someone who works here." Women around the room nodded and laughed in recognition.

"How many people in the room are having that same problem right now?" I asked. Dozens of hands went up.

The culture at this firm was tough. It was highly competitive, and feedback was given in an insensitive way. Most of the women in the room had an internalized inner critic that was reflective of the firm's culture—and in particular, reflective of a few harsh senior voices in the company.

If, as you've been reading this chapter, you've noticed that your inner critic sounds like an internalized voice of a family member or professional colleague or boss, you can use this to your advantage. You know something about this person's struggles and fears. You can probably see some of the wounds in their own life that led to the beliefs that you've internalized as an inner critic. You can shine the light of understanding on your critic even more brightly because of your familiarity with this person.

Second, don't blame. It's not this person's fault that you grapple with self-doubt. Remember that we are hardwired for the critic: If your inner critic didn't find inspiration in your mother, your father, or your boss, it would have found it elsewhere.

And third, don't preach. Especially with family members, you might feel tempted to go tell them about your new discovery of your inner critic and what they had to do with it! Not a good move. The best way you can be of service to both your own growth and to theirs is to focus on your own inner work. They will be more influenced by who you become than by what you try to tell them.

Getting to Know Your
Inner Critic—Journaling Questions

· ·

Write down some of the things that your inner critic says. What are its commonly voiced beliefs? If you are having trouble thinking of what it says, here are some situations that may prompt your answers:

- *What—if anything—does it say to you when you contemplate speaking up about something that feels scary or like a stretch during an important meeting at work?*
- *When you think about making a career move that excites you?*
- *When you come up with a big idea?*
- *About starting a website or blog of some kind?*
- *When you walk into a party where you don't know many people?*
- *When you are feeling challenged as a parent, wife, or daughter?*
- *About reclaiming a creative hobby or sharing your creative work with others?*
- *When you're getting dressed in the morning?*
- *When you look in the mirror?*

- *When you are trying on clothes in a store or getting dressed for an important event?*

Sometimes, our inner critics take "inspiration" from people in our lives—that abusive boss from years ago, the mean advisor from graduate school, a tough family member. Does your inner critic echo any external critics?

Sometimes, our inner critics have cultural sources. For example, you might see your inner critic as the archetype of "the perfect Southern wife" or "the ideal daughter in Chinese culture." What cultural archetypes does your inner critic embody or ask you to live up to?

Looking over your inner critic's common narratives, brainstorm five adjectives that describe your inner critic's personality. For example, maybe your inner critic is hyper or anxious or people-pleasing or stubborn.

Create a character. Bring your inner critic's voice to mind. Notice: Does it sound like a female voice or a male voice? An older voice or a younger voice? From there, start to imagine: If your inner critic were a person, what kind of person would it be? An old, stern professor? The popular girl in high school?

Create a character who personifies your inner critic. You can invent a character or pick a figure from film, literature, politics, or pop culture. Build out a portrait of his or her life: Where does your critic live? What does he or she wear? What does he or she eat for breakfast? Name your character and begin to call it by its name when it shows up.

Lisa Jemus, a student in my Playing Big program, put it this way: "My inner critic is an older female. She is in a dark kitchen with this fringy lamp lighting her. She's got the long fingernails and the red lipstick and the dark, dyed hair. She's got a crackly sort of voice, and she's quite mean. I named her Sharza. When I wrote her name again at the end of all the describing, I wrote, 'Hah, what a joke!' I thought, 'She doesn't even know what she's talking about.' That's really what I felt in that moment, and I had never felt that before about this voice in me. That was a gift. I look at her with quite a bit of humor actually. The whole thing is quite funny."

Here's how Rebekah described hers: "I named my inner critic 'Slave Driver.' She has harsh, angular features and dishwater blond hair. She's super intense, high energy, muscular. She's always in motion, always demanding more. She carries a whip at her hip and drives a very fast red car. It's kind of fun to laugh at it now that I got it written all out there. She's bitter over her past and wants to project that on me. She keeps herself safe by living by strict rules and wants to impose them on me also. She's trying to keep me busy, always pushing me to be more, do more. There is something deep within her that she's never dealt with that she copes with by being busy, projecting her pain and need for busyness onto me."

You may find that your inner critic has a few different voices. For example, one critic voice might sound like a former ceramics teacher and show up around your pottery, one might worry about disappointing people and so pushes you to overcommit, and one might get really cynical and nasty and give up on things abruptly. That's great—you're refining your understanding of how the inner critic operates in your life. You can untangle the thread of your inner critic into several different strands. Kellie McElhaney, a professor at UC Berkeley's Haas School of Business, talks about her two inner critics:

"I have two inner critics. One is a personal life inner critic and one is a professional life inner critic. The personal life inner critic is Heather from the film *Heathers*. The professional inner critic is the stereotypical old, male professor. In my mind he looks like Ebenezer Scrooge. Interestingly, they often cross over out of their area of expertise. The personal inner critic, Heather, will criticize me about things on the job (about which she knows nothing), and the professor will criticize me about my personal life."

Journal about your inner critic character. What's he or she like? What would his or her name be?

How does personifying the critic lighten its influence and help you take it less seriously? How does it help you see it as simply one voice within— not the whole of you or the real you?

Investigate your critic's motives. Think of something that your inner critic is talking to you about at this stage of your life. Close your eyes. Picture the character that you've created. Hear the inner critic saying that thing it says. Then, in your mind's eye, ask him or her, "Why are you saying that to me? What are you trying to achieve by saying that?"

Write a sincere "thank you, but no thank you" note to the inner critic. Here is an example:

Dear Perfectionista—I feel your pain! Life can be so stressful, and I know you believe strongly that if we just work really hard, if we just do an excellent job, life will be safe, and people will like us. You have helped us get good results in lots of situations. And your work ethic is incredible! Right now, however, I am going to try another approach. I'm okay without you in this situation. Thanks so much for trying to protect me, as always. I'll see you later. —Jeannie

If you're motivated in part by your critic, look back: When in your life did you experience a lot of motivation that didn't come from fear and self-doubt? What motivated you then? How did acting from that place feel, and what were the results?

Friendly Warning:
Inner Critic Work Is Ongoing

As you use the tools and journaling questions in this chapter, you'll find your relationship with your inner critic begins to change. But no matter how amazing your initial results, don't think you are done! The critic will be back. Remember the function of the critic: to try to keep you safe from any emotional risk, even those emotional risks you want to take on the road to playing bigger. It will speak up when you stretch in new ways. Come back to the tools and journaling questions again and again as you need them.

The inner critic is a crafty, rapidly evolving entity. Let's say your inner critic used to show up with messages pressuring you to work long hours. You successfully became aware of it and are reducing your hours and valuing your free time. You can expect to hear the inner critic show up with the opposite message—that you are not doing a good enough job reducing hours and valuing your free time! It will work itself into your new framework; it will use the currency of what you value at any given moment. When you learn to recognize your inner critic's usual lines, it will invent new ones and come at you from a different angle. So, expect to use inner critic management tools in an ongoing way in your life. These are practices for forever.

The Big Ideas

1. Having an inner critic is neither abnormal nor pathological. We *all* have inner critics.

2. The critic is one voice in you—a voice that may have become dominant. But it's not the core you. The core you is the you of your talents, your aspirations, and your desire to express and receive love in the world in your unique way.

3. The goal isn't to get rid of your inner critic. The goal is to learn how to hear those crazy thoughts and self-doubts, know them for what they are, and not let them determine what you do.

4. The inner critic is worried about keeping you safe. It doesn't care at all whether you are fulfilled along the way. If you listen to the critic, you'll take fewer risks of a certain kind, but you won't make the contribution you are meant to make.

5. The foundational tool for dealing with the inner critic is this: Recognize the inner critic when it shows up and name it for what it is.

CHAPTER 2

• • •

The Voice of Inner Wisdom

I feel as if I'm about to let you in on a priceless secret. Again and again, the women I work with tell me that this is the practice that has made the most dramatic difference in their lives and work.

I first encountered it when I was studying at the Coaches Training Institute. In one of my initial workshops there, the teachers led us through a visualization exercise they called "future self." They dimmed the lights, asked us to close our eyes, get comfortable, take some deep breaths, and relax. Then, for about twenty minutes, they narrated as each of us visualized traveling to earth twenty years in the future. We met our future selves, the woman or man we'd become twenty years from now.

The teachers led us step by step to arriving at his or her home, and asked us to notice: What kind of place did she live in? What was her presence like? Who was the woman who greeted us at the door? They told us to have a chat with this older self, to ask him or her questions like "What do I need to know to get from where I am to where you are?" and "What has been most important about the past twenty years?" We could ask this future self about any dilemma in our lives and see what he or she had to say about it. Then they guided us to bring the conversation to an end and to imagine ourselves traveling back to earth in the present day.

We opened our eyes and, in the silence, wrote down what we'd each seen in the visualization. Then, several of the students shared about their experiences. Most had been extremely moved by the future self they'd met. A business executive in his sixties who had seemed emotionally numb through the course thus far cried profusely as he talked about his older self. A mom of four who usually was exhausted and stressed seemed rejuvenated and calm. As people spoke about their experiences, it became clear: The future selves they encountered were not really just older versions of themselves. They were more like guides, mentors with incredible wisdom, figures who imparted a sense of peace and integrity so profound it could hardly be put into words. They'd met individuals who weren't merely older selves but more authentic, fully expressed versions of themselves. In these "future selves" all their best qualities and gifts shone brightly.

The teachers explained that this was an exercise we could do with our coaching clients to help them uncover visions for their future and a sense of their more fulfilled, authentic selves.

My Inner Mentor

That day when I first did the "future self" visualization, things didn't go so well for me. My classmates were having poignant, joyful experiences, but I was not. When the teachers asked us to see the home of our future self, I saw a small, ramshackle, decaying house.

A haggard, depleted woman came to the door. She wore a tattered apron over a faded housedress, no makeup, no jewelry, and her uncared-for hair fell around her face. She looked so tired, so beaten down, so sad. I immediately had the sense that the reason for all that was because she had put everyone else's needs before her own for the twenty years that stood between me and her. There was simply nothing left of her. When I asked her the questions the teachers told us to ask our future selves, rather than providing me with wisdom, she tearfully asked me for help, for rescue.

I was disappointed. Everyone else in the room—all my fellow coaches-in-training—were sharing epiphanies and accounts of the inspiring visions they'd encountered. What did this mean for me and for my future? I tentatively raised my hand: "What if you have a negative experience?" I described what I had seen.

"Well, *that* won't do," my teacher Carla immediately said. She guided me through a shortened form of the exercise again, this time in front of the whole class. This second time, I saw a very different picture. The woman I saw lived in a house by the sea, next to roaring waves. She was a writer. That came as a total surprise at the time, because I wasn't doing any writing then and hadn't written for years. But this woman? Writing was at the center of her life and her work.

Her home and personal style had a Zen-like simplicity mine didn't. I noticed a short, very neat to-do list on a small pad on her empty kitchen counter, with a great black ink pen. I was always losing pens, writing with crappy ones and being annoyed by it, and keeping way too many piles of paper around. I had the sense that she'd simplified her life and her daily routine, dramatically.

Her appearance exuded a kind of earthy femininity—long, flowing hair, soft colors—nothing like the trousers and blazers I wore to work every day. I could tell that her spirituality was at the center of her life. I was in a kind of spiritual dry spell. She was clearly also an artist and, her legs showed me, a dancer. My passions for art and dance had been neglected for many years. And she lived in a house by the sea. She could see and hear ocean waves from her windows. I lived in a house . . . by the freeway.

I recognized her: She was a composite of all the most important parts of me that I had left behind. I got the message. The first depressing picture showed me the waste of a life I'd end up having if I continued my worst people-pleasing behaviors and kept doing only those things that were in my small comfort zone or that were acceptable to others.

The woman in my second visualization felt both unfamiliar and familiar. Some parts of her I immediately knew were buried parts of myself. Other aspects of her life and home felt more surprising and mysterious—the minimalism, the simplicity, a kind of feeling of solitude. I had the sense this woman represented, in a not-quite-literal form, the woman I was at my core and the woman I was meant to be.

In the months that followed, I began growing into her. I started writing again and I held myself to one standard: trying to write the kind of work she would write—more honest, brave, and unconventional words than I would have written had I not had her in mind. I picked up my old favorite spiritual books and began reading them again in the early mornings, rekindling my spiritual life. I bought a few things in the kinds of colors and fabrics she wore in my imagined vision of her. I grew out my hair to resemble hers.

One morning, sitting alone in the silence of 5:00 A.M., I looked around my living room and realized there was only *one* object in the room—an unusual chair made out of a tamarind tree trunk—that she would have had in her home. Only *one thing* reflected her style—which of course was my true taste and style, which I hadn't yet had the courage to express in my house. Everything else in my living room was way too square, too conventional for her and, really, for me. When I had seen that chair, I'd fallen in love with it—it was so sculptural, unusual, elemental. I adored it and felt so good having it in my home. I started to consider the possibility, which then seemed radical, that I could create a home full of things I loved as much as that tamarind chair.

These choices—seemingly superficial ones like furniture and clothes, and deeper ones like reclaiming my creative passions—mingled together as day by day I kept asking, "Well, which choice here—*a* or *b*—will bring me closer to living her life?" I'd choose whichever option, whichever action, did that. In those months of transition, when I looked in the mirror, or at my living room, or in my calendar, and saw more and more of her expressed in my present life, it showed me, yes, you can become that amazing woman you met in the vision. In fact, you *are* becoming her.

This is the very heart of playing bigger: having the vision of a more authentic, fully expressed, free-from-fear you and growing more and more into her, being *pulled* by this resonant vision rather than *pushing* to achieve markers of success.

Coaching Women to Discover Their Inner Mentors

After learning about the "future self" tool in my coaching training, I began using it with my clients. When I'd do the visualization exercise with them, the results were always remarkable. Truly *remarkable.* No matter how confused, afraid, or lost the person sitting in my office was, the future self she'd meet would be very different:

unfailingly wise, entirely loving. That future self would offer an entirely different—and incredibly helpful—perspective on her challenges and dilemmas.

As my work evolved to focus on helping women play bigger, I found the future self to be an indispensable tool. It allowed women to find their own right answers again and again. I began to call it the inner mentor because I found this voice functioned for women as a source of guidance, a voice women could draw on to develop a vision for their lives and careers, to make difficult decisions, to chart their paths. It also served as a counterpoint to the inner critic voice many women hear so loudly. A woman might come into the office hearing mainly her inner critic's rants and raves about something—an upcoming salary negotiation, a difficult conversation with a colleague, an important presentation—but by imagining how her future self would approach it, she'd become confident and have a clear sense of what to say and do. Or a woman would come in feeling stuck about how to pursue her dream career and, by imagining what her future self would do, could immediately see a path forward that felt just right to her but that she hadn't thought of before. My job as a coach became less about advising or even supporting and more about giving women the tools to recognize when their inner critics were talking and to ask their inner mentors for their input instead.

Often the inner mentor's answers are surprising. A woman would be considering two options, and her inner mentor would offer a third, previously unconsidered possibility, an out-of-the-box idea that "clicked" for her. Or her inner mentor would give her a sense of humor about the thing she was upset about, showing her why it wasn't a big deal. Or her inner mentor would offer an extremely simple answer like "Focus on love" or "Trust the process"—

words that seemed clichéd from the outside but were, in fact, very helpful and comforting because they were delivered with such presence and verity from the voice within.

After working with thousands of women, I know that every woman has an incredible inner mentor inside of her, a voice that has the just-right-for-her answers at every turn. She simply needs to learn how to discover this voice and to be reminded to access it regularly, until that becomes her habitual way of doing things.

From Inner Critic to Inner Mentor

After several years working in human resources, Diana went back to school to become a nutritionist and start her own business. In the early months of her new career, she was plagued by self-doubt. Her inner critic relentlessly asked, "Why would anyone work with a newbie like you, when there are so many experienced nutritionists out there? And what are you offering that's so different?" In its most cruel moments, that voice in her head would say, "How can you purport to help people with food issues when you still turn to eating ice cream when you are feeling upset? And who is going to hire a health coach with a body like yours?"

Through her work in the Playing Big course, Diana developed a sense of her inner mentor, an imagined version of herself twenty years out into the future. "She's comfortable in her own skin and with her age, with stunning silvery-white hair," Diana said. "She has a kind of calm about her that is so reassuring. She has a thriving business, thriving not in that she's famous or making millions, but in that she gets to do the work she really loves, make a good living, and know she has made a difference in the lives of her clients, whom she adores. She paints and her house is full of her paintings, including many scenes from her family life over the years. It's interesting because painting is something I loved in childhood but haven't thought about in a long time."

Diana got a sense of who this woman was, how she lived her life, and what her presence was like. Then Diana began to check in with that inner mentor voice within her whenever she faced a difficult dilemma or got stuck in her business. She'd ask herself, "How would my inner mentor approach launching a health coaching business? How would this calm, confident, loving woman go about the process of getting new clients? How would her website look? Her branding?"

Diana developed her business in this way, exploring how her inner mentor would go about each task or project—especially those that she felt afraid or confused about. Diana said, "Before, I was letting my inner critic be in charge of the process of deciding on my target market, designing my website, and writing my materials, and I kept getting stuck, feeling afraid, and hating what I was producing. Then, I put my inner mentor in charge and just kept doing what I thought *she* would do. The result is a business that truly reflects me. That has made the business much more differentiated, and it's drawing a unique group of clients who really appreciate what I have to offer."

Like Diana, Colleen Haggerty, an author and former nonprofit executive, was able to replace her inner critic's fears with her inner mentor's confidence. She told this story about her inner mentor:

"Last summer, during the Playing Big course, I applied to my local TEDx event. Of the one hundred applicants, just eighteen were selected as speakers. When I read the e-mail that I was one of the eighteen chosen, I was elated.

"About a month later, the TEDx committee facilitated a daylong workshop for the speakers. Up until that day, this had been a solo experience and I felt confident and sure of myself. But once I knew I had to face the other presenters, I felt scared. 'Who do you think you are?' my inner critic screamed as I drove to the workshop. 'Everyone else has something of value to say. Just go home now.'

" 'Where are you?' I asked my inner mentor.

" 'Here I am,' she said with a strong, deep, comforting voice. 'Colleen, everything in your life has led you to this moment. Right here, right now. You are meant to be here. What you have to say needs to be said. There are so many people who need to hear your message in just the way you need to say it. This is your sacred work. Do not go home. Walk into that room and claim your space.'

"We each went up to the front of the room and gave the first thirty seconds of our TEDx talks. I walked to the front, took a deep breath, and I felt like I embodied my inner mentor. I was calm, sure, and unapologetic. What I most appreciated is that my inner mentor guided me into that room—a place where I would normally compare, and then fall into despair—with a firm understanding of my uniqueness.

"I heeded my inner mentor's words during the following six weeks before the TEDx event. Every time I practiced the talk before a group, I kept my inner mentor's thoughts tucked into my heart: 'There are people who need to hear what I have to say. What I have to say needs to be said. This is my sacred work.' After every practice session, at least one person talked to me about how powerful my message was for him or her.

"When the day finally came, I walked up on the TEDx stage, hand in hand with my inner mentor, claimed the space as my own, and I gave the talk of my life."

Listening to the inner mentor instead of the inner critic is the first of the major shifts that enable us to move from playing small to playing big. We move from giving our attention to the inner critic voice to giving it to the inner mentor voice, from taking direction from the critic to receiving the wisdom of the inner mentor.

Becoming a Change Agent

Claudia is an MD/PhD with a prestigious job as a researcher at one of the most elite scientific institutions in the country. "There's another team across the country researching the exact same topic as my group," Claudia told me one day. "The two labs don't talk to each other. The field is so competitive, that's just the norm. But it feels so wrong to me. By not communicating about our studies, we create redundancy and waste research dollars. Plus, we're both shooting ourselves in the foot: Either both teams will come out with the same findings, or we'll have conflicting, potentially confusing findings because we are using different data and methods to investigate the same question. Either outcome will be bad for all our careers. If we simply coordinate enough to use either the same data with different methods or the same methods with different data, the research we each do we will be more meaningful to the field."

In the Playing Big course, Claudia developed a clear picture and sense of her inner mentor. So, we explored what Claudia's inner mentor would do about the situation with the other research lab. Claudia immediately saw that her inner mentor could carve a path through the dysfunctional culture of her field. She would rise above it. Her inner mentor would think about what was in the best interest of kids' health—the focus of her research—and do whatever was aligned with that.

Claudia said, "Checking in with my inner mentor helped me settle my nerves. Then I decided to do what she would do. I called the other head researcher and talked with him about us mutually sharing our methods as we do the research, so it isn't a disaster when we both publish and so that we can potentially produce something that is a greater contribution to the field. At first he was taken aback, but after talking for a while, he seemed to trust me and my intentions. We've been moving forward with a more collaborative approach and it's helping both of our projects." Claudia's story is a powerful example of what so many women experience: Their inner mentor shows them how to step out of the norms of their time and place and be courageous change agents, transforming their institutions and industries to be more enlightened.

Simple Answers

Our inner mentor keeps things simple. When we overcomplicate a situation, she helps us see the bottom line. When we think it has to be hard, she shows us how it can be easy. Sandy Johnson Clark, an executive at a career management firm, describes her experience:

> "I have always loved to write. The phrase *get published* showed up every year on my list of annual goals. Playing big held but one aspiration for me—getting published—yet I just wasn't able to take action on it. I asked my inner mentor what was most surprising about how she approached her

writing career and she said, 'It's not so much work. This can be easy.' The clarity I had about what I should do next was astonishing. I started to write about a topic on which I was an expert. I composed a piece that flowed so easily that my fingers could hardly keep up with the speed of my thoughts. After some very minor editing, I submitted it with confidence to a business editor at Forbes.com. No small-town publication for me. I was going for the mass media! Not two hours after I submitted it, an affirmative response appeared in my inbox. My inner mentor *showed me that I was ready and that it could be simple to do this*. She knows me best. I just have to listen."

Many women experience what Sandy, Colleen, and Diana have: Their inner mentors enable them to play bigger and achieve more, but not in the traditional way. Our inner mentors don't ask us to strive more, work harder, or push. Instead, they show us a simpler, easier, but highly effective—and authentic—way forward.

Inner and Outer Mentors

No one wants to cry in their company conference room—certainly not in front of dozens of their colleagues. But on this particular day, I'd made several women well up with tears at work, without meaning to. I was giving a talk for women at a Silicon Valley technology company. During the Q&A period, a woman asked a question about her next professional steps. She was considering a few different career paths, each with pros and cons. She described the options and asked if I had any advice. I couldn't answer her question directly, because of course only she could know the answer about what step was right for her, but I could help her find her own answer.

I introduced the group to the "inner mentor" concept and guided them through a short visualization exercise of meeting their older, wiser selves. When we finished the visualization, I looked into the audience and saw a number of the women had tears in their eyes. "I'm surprised how emotional I'm getting," one of them said. "It's just that no one has ever talked to me about a voice like this before. It's so comforting to think that instead of having to find the right mentor or find the right answer 'out there' somewhere, I could actually find it within myself."

It's so true: Most of us haven't been taught much about this whole, wise part of ourselves. Rochelle, a consultant to nonprofit organizations, put it this way: "I had long been aware of my inner critic. In therapy, you focus on the inner critic side of things. I knew about the snarky, wounded little girl voice in me, but I didn't know about this other voice, the already whole part of me, the inner mentor." In part, we are more familiar with the inner critic than the inner mentor because we hear the inner critic voice more loudly. The inner critic demands our attention. The inner mentor waits to be paid attention to. Where the inner critic rants and raves, the inner mentor speaks softly. The inner critic interrupts and invades our thinking. The inner mentor almost always waits to be asked for input before she speaks.

I asked the woman who had originally posed the question what her inner mentor would say about her career path dilemma. I waited as she checked in with that older, wiser self. "It's interesting," she said. "She's kind of chuckling at me, about how much I've been trying to plan this out. She's telling me to just keep putting one foot in front of the other and doing my best work in my current role, that the answer will become clear if I do that." To an outsider, this might sound like an easy answer, but the woman who experienced it didn't feel that way about it at all. She experienced relief and a new way of approaching her next steps.

It is a sad state of affairs when women find it a surprising, moving idea that they can turn inward to access their own wisdom to navigate their careers. Though dressed in the guise of women's empowerment, all the encouragement for women to find the right mentors and right advice is often, underneath, the same old message telling them to turn away from their own intuitions and wisdom and to privilege the guidance coming from others instead. As Sheryl Sandberg writes in *Lean In*, ". . . searching for a mentor has become the professional equivalent of waiting for Prince Charming. We all grew up on the fairy tale 'Sleeping Beauty,' which instructs young women that if they just wait for their prince to arrive, they will be kissed and whisked away on a white horse to live happily ever after. Now young women are told that if they can just find the right mentor, they will be pushed up the ladder and whisked away to the corner office to live happily ever after. Once again, we are teaching women to be too dependent on others."

Women are enjoined again and again to seek external resources to help their careers, but they aren't encouraged as frequently to trust their own instincts and find their own answers inside. As part of this, women are endlessly told to seek "outer" mentors—*other* people who can show us the way, make connections, and give us advice. But frequently I hear women talking about the limitations of those mentoring relationships: Younger women can't find the mentors they seek, often because female leaders in their fields are so few or so overtaxed. Or, when they look at those leaders, they don't see careers or lives they want to emulate, and the advice they receive from them simply doesn't resonate. Many women have had painful experiences when mentors—male or female—felt threatened by them and didn't provide support or, worse, betrayed or undermined them. Plus, mentoring entails a hierarchical relationship that doesn't appeal to many women today, who gravitate more toward mutually supportive relationships with two-way exchanges of expertise and opportunities.

The traditional mentor-mentee hierarchical relationship is particularly tricky for women as they step into playing bigger, because that often involves their pioneering *new* ways of crafting their lives and careers or acting as change agents in their organizations or communities. As innovators, their primary need is not for someone who went before them who can show them the ropes and give advice based on what worked for them. Rather, they need tools and encouragement to find their own unprecedented ways forward.

Your inner mentor can give you a kind of support that no outer mentor can give you. She's not a replacement for outer mentors, but she is a necessary complement to them. Because she's inside of you, she'll always be there for you, unfailingly. There are no issues of competition or betrayal. And because she's *your* inner voice, her guidance won't be a reflection of what worked for someone else; it will always be just right for you. What is most important about the inner mentor is that she liberates you from playing big on anyone else's terms and shows you what playing big really looks like for you.

There's a quote that's wildly popular right now in the women's empowerment conversation: "You can't be what you can't see." We need role models, these words tell us, for whatever we aim to become. "You can't be what you can't see" has gone over so well with audiences that, as of this writing, there are *1.7 million* citations of the quote on the web. But the popularity of this phrase shows how much we've forgotten about the role of inner vision. *Of course* we can be what we can't see. It is how every important "first" has happened—because someone was able to become something she had never seen before. A woman who opens a business when no woman in her village has ever done it; a woman who decides to be the first to run for president in her country; a woman who is the first person she knows to leave an abusive marriage—all these women had to be something they had never seen before.

Perhaps a better—though less snappy—mantra would be, "We can't be what we can't imagine." We can't be what we can't see in our own inner vision.

My childhood dance teacher, Judith Komoroske, is one of the wisest and most brilliant women I know. A gifted dancer, she is also a painter, a poet, a mother of three grown daughters, and a grandmother. Now in her seventies, she's learning to play musical instruments she'd never touched before.

We meet up from time to time for a chat and a cup of tea. Over one of those cups of chamomile, I talked to her about the phenomenon I saw in myself and in the women around me: the self-doubt, the playing small.

"Well, of course," she said. "That's because American women are liberated but not empowered."

I was stunned. Quite a statement, delivered off the cuff as if it were the most obvious thing in the world. I found that idea, that American women are liberated but not yet empowered, profoundly resonant.

"Why do you think that is?" I asked her. "Why are we struggling so much with the empowerment part?"

She gave an answer I'd never heard before and have never heard anywhere since.

"It's a failure of imagination. If people haven't been taught how to use their creativity, how to *imagine*, then they can't create a dramatically different reality than what they know today, because they can't imagine it."

It was an artist's answer. Typically, we speak about many other factors that keep women from fully claiming our freedoms: persistent bias, media images, stress, self-doubt, work-family balance issues. Judith spoke to a linchpin of social and personal change often overlooked: imagination. Inner vision.

The inner mentor gives us a specific, vibrant, compelling vision so that we don't have to depend on what we can *see* to prescribe what we can *be*. In this historical moment of women unleashing their voices and—we hope—changing the world as they do, we can't depend on what we can see outside ourselves to show us the way. The personal and collective transformation we need to enact is too different from what exists. We are called to forge significant reimaginings, restructurings, reconceptualizing of the status quo. What is required will come from within as much as from without.

What Is the Inner Mentor?

After seeing so many women experience their inner mentors as vivid, living presences with personalities and consistency over time, after seeing how powerful the inner mentor voice was in helping them play bigger, I began to wonder, What was this inner voice? What is this part of us that sees things so differently than we see them in our day-to-day consciousness? What were women really drawing on when they drew on this voice?

I don't think there is literally an "inner mentor" character inside each of us, but I do believe—because I've seen it in thousands of women now—that there is a voice in each of us that is unburdened by fear and untouched by insecurity, that has utter calm, that emanates love for oneself and others, and that knows *exactly* who we would be if we were brave enough to show up as our true selves. The "inner mentor" is a way of accessing that part of us, a tool to tap into it. It can then become one's personal guide to playing bigger.

You can think of your inner mentor as a part of you that is whole, centered, loving. You can think of her as a vision of the woman you are growing into, a vision of a more evolved future self. You can think of your inner mentor as the voice of your spirit or soul, if those terms resonate for you. I believe she is all these.

Growing into Your Inner Mentor

We begin to grow into our inner mentors by asking simple, concrete questions like these: What does she like to do first thing in the morning? How does she like to spend an evening? What kind of meals does she love to have? What kind of exercise or physical activity does she do, and what's the attitude she takes toward it? How does she rest? How does she behave at family or social gatherings? What kind of clothes does she wear? We can ask again and again, "How does she approach *this*?" and walk as if in her shoes.

Then there are the bigger shifts. Before a difficult conversation we can ask ourselves, "What would she say?" and say just that. We can pause as we're writing an important piece of correspondence to consider, "How would she write this?" We can see how she'd handle a messy relationship situation, a dysfunctional work environment, a potential career move, a paralyzing fear, or a persistent issue in ourselves we've failed to resolve for years. Gerd Nilsson, a Playing Big course graduate, describes her practice: "I have made it a habit to meet my inner mentor for a conversation in the morning when I mentally prepare for the day ahead. If there are any particularly challenging issues I will have to deal with, I ask her how she would deal with it. And all of a sudden I just know."

We can consult with her on decisions too. After I met my inner mentor, when I was faced with an important decision, I'd ask myself, which of these roads moves me closer to becoming that woman I saw in the visualization? That criteria helped me quickly say a lot of nos and some significant yeses. It helped me tune out external pressures and helped me find the answers that were right for me.

You don't ever fully become your inner mentor. She's not a destination at which you arrive. Rather, she's a North Star you can keep looking to, a way to navigate your path, a touchstone to return to again and again in the face of tough choices and challenging moments.

Discovering Your Inner Mentor

I'm guessing that as you've been reading this chapter, you've been skeptical—skeptical that you really have a voice of perfect wisdom inside, that you could access it as readily as the women in these stories seemed to. I assure you, they were skeptical too. And if you simply try to ask yourself, Hmm, what would my older self do?, you'll likely get an unsatisfying answer. To get to your real inner mentor, you simply have to take time to slow down and do the visualization. Otherwise, you'll just be working with a fantasy about your future—not that deeper voice of wisdom.

Doing the guided visualization will allow you to go beyond your intellectual ideas or conscious hopes for what the future "you" looks like to that miraculous and unfailing inner voice. Two good criteria to use are these: (1) If you aren't genuinely moved by the image and presence of the inner mentor you see in your mind's eye, and (2) if she does not have a significantly different view from you about the various challenges in your current life, then you haven't really accessed her voice yet. The visualization will help you truly get to her.

After the visualization, use the journaling questions that follow to record what you discovered and then to more fully flesh out the "portrait" of your inner mentor.

To discover your inner mentor, go to www.taramohr.com /pbbookmaterials, where you can listen to an audio file that will guide you through the visualization to meet her. The visualization is also included in written form in the pages that follow. However, be sure to do the audio or have a trustworthy support person in your life read the text to you so that you can close your eyes and actually *do* the visualization.

If You Get Stuck . . .

Sometimes, women do the visualization and tell me they got stuck or "it didn't work" for them. I've learned over the years that quite often women feel as if there was something wrong or lacking with what they saw in their visualizations, when in fact there really wasn't.

If you feel surprised or uncomfortable about what showed up in your visualization, frustrated that your inner mentor didn't answer some of your questions more clearly, your mind occasionally wandered, or some elements of the visualization were very vague or missing entirely, this is all just fine! None of those qualify as "getting stuck" or the exercise not working. Surprises mean you accessed something beyond your conscious plans and desires—that's a good thing. Things that made you uncomfortable may simply depart from your ego's plans and show you something important and unexpected about yourself. Occasional mind wandering and some vague or absent aspects of the vision are no problem.

On the other hand, if you fell asleep, were distracted to the extent that you missed much of the visualization, or you saw a dark and depressing picture of your future, give the visualization a second try, as I did.

Here are a few additional suggestions if you got stuck:

- If you felt agitated or distracted during the visualization, take some steps to slow down more beforehand when you try it again. Take a bath, drink some tea, dim the lights—do whatever helps you physically relax.
- If your challenge was being too relaxed (falling asleep), try sitting up in a chair rather than lying down, and pick a time of day when you'll be alert.
- If your challenge was seeing an inner critic–ridden version of your inner mentor, go to chapter 1, use some of the inner critic tools outlined there, and then give the visualization a second try.

Another thing that can help is to vary the journey. Instead of traveling on beams of light (if that part didn't work for you), see yourself taking a long mountain hike or sailing across a lake to meet your inner mentor.

Sometimes, women find that visualization just doesn't work for them. If you've tried the visualization a couple of times and stayed stuck, change up the medium. Make a collage about your inner mentor, and let your intuition guide what images you pick. Choose ones that don't "make any sense" but that you feel pulled toward. Or journal about your inner mentor. Get comfortable, turn off your phone, and take some deep breaths, relaxing any tension throughout your body. Then journal. To really slow down and get out of your head, you can even write the journaling questions from your current self that are included below in your dominant hand (whichever hand you usually write with), and change to your nondominant hand when writing the answers from your inner mentor.

INTERPRETING YOUR INNER MENTOR VISION

- **Explore symbols.** Often, when women encounter their inner mentor in the guided visualization, they ask me questions like "It was a little odd, but my husband didn't seem to live in my inner mentor's house—does that mean that I'm not married anymore?" or "I didn't seem to have a career—my inner mentor just spent her time at the beach and cooking up amazing meals in her kitchen. But I love my career, and I don't cook!" Often, these elements aren't literal but metaphors or symbols. To understand the symbols in your inner mentor vision, ask yourself, "What associations do I have with this place, activity, or object in the visualization? What did it seem to connote to me? What was the feeling or tone it had in the visualization?"

- **Don't try to pin down an interpretation of what you saw in your visualization.** It can be tempting to try to figure out what the vision meant. "Am I *really* going to end up moving to the jungle? Am I actually going to become a teacher? Am I going to have five kids?" Don't go down that road. You won't find answers to those questions through thinking about them. Live with the imagery and feelings that came through your visualization for a while. Their meanings will reveal themselves to you over time.

- **Be open to all the ways your inner mentor communicates.** Your internal mentor may speak to you in words or simply through her facial expressions, body language, or the energy of her presence. Or she may mostly communicate to you through the symbols in the visualization—like the parting gift or her home. Be open to however she is communicating with you rather than wanting something more concrete or obvious.

- **Look up your inner mentor's name.** In the visualization, your inner mentor gave you a name for her true essence. Often, women will hear a name or word with which they have no familiarity or a term they don't know the meaning of. Look up the root and meaning of the word or name online. What does it suggest to you about your inner mentor?

- **Keep your inner mentor close.** A few years ago, I attended a writing retreat led by my friend, author Jen Louden. On the last morning of the week-long retreat, Jen gave us a number of guidelines for "reentry" into our regular lives. She told us *not* to recount the retreat experience to our friends or spouses. Jen explained that time and time again she'd seen attempts to do so go wrong, that what we go through in these kinds of intensive, personal growth experiences can't be summarized in words and is rarely met with the kind of reverence and understanding from others that we desire and that the experience deserves. Our translations fall flat, others' reactions feel disappointing—if not hurtful—and we're left feeling as if somehow the experience became less sacred or real or magical because of our telling it. The same thing is true of your inner mentor visualization. Your verbal summary won't do it justice and others will likely respond in a way that will feel like a letdown. My suggestion is this: Keep alive your experience of your visualization in your own heart and mind, but keep it to yourself, at least for a while. Then be very thoughtful about whom you choose to tell about your experience.

FUTURE SELF GUIDED VISUALIZATION
From the Coaches Training Institute

Find a comfortable spot where you can sit—a comfy chair or sofa is great—or recline in bed. Have a pen and paper nearby, as you'll do some writing by hand right after the visualization.

Close your eyes. Take a few deep breaths. Relax all the little muscles around your eyes. Release your jaw. Let your cheeks feel heavy. Notice your breath as you inhale and exhale, inhale and exhale.

Imagine that your body is a body of water, a calm lake. As you take a breath in and release it out, just notice the soft current in that body of water. Let each exhale carry some tension and stress away. And again with another breath out, just let any tension or stress float away.

Bring your attention to your feet. Notice if you're carrying any tightness or stress in your feet, and if so, just soften there, let it out. Let a soft heaviness come into your feet. Move your attention to your calves, your shins, and relax that area; send some breath there to loosen it up. Soften around your knees, breathing in and out and relaxing more deeply. Now move your attention upward, releasing your quads and upper legs. Imagine any tension that's there seeping away.

Then as you take your next inhalation, imagine your breath moving into your hips, into your pelvic area, and opening it up. As you exhale, let any stress and tension melt away. Let your belly fully release. Relax your torso and your chest. Let any stress seep out of it. Now move your attention to your upper back and your shoulders; let any tension melt right off and down your back and soften your neck, your jaw, and your tongue. Relax your brow. Let go of any tension you're holding there. Release your upper arms, your lower arms, your hands.

Now, bring your attention to the spot on your forehead right between your eyes. Notice a beam of light stretching out from that point on your forehead. Notice if that beam of light has a color or set of colors in it. Notice the quality of that light. Notice that this beam of light stretches all the way up out of the room that you're in, out above and through the ceiling. Notice that it actually stretches all the way up out of the building that you're in, and shines out into the sky.

Start to travel along this beam of light. Start to imagine floating up and just let yourself walk along that beam up out of the room where you are, following the beam upward. Allow that beam to take you higher and higher. Notice the building where you were getting smaller in your view. As you travel, notice the beauty of the sky and move through the clouds. Start to see the view of your city or town below you.

As you travel faster and higher, start to see the whole region where you were beneath you. Move up and up until you can see the beautiful globe of blue and green and white, and enjoy the view. Travel upward and upward until you're in blue-black space—silent, velvety, and dark.

Notice that there is another beam next to the one that you are standing on, another beam of light. Notice what the color and quality of that beam is. Notice that this beam stretches all the way back down toward Earth. Notice that this beam stretches down toward Earth twenty years into the future, twenty years from now. Go ahead and step onto that beam and let it gracefully carry you down. Notice Earth starting to come into focus again—the contours starting to get clearer and larger in your view. Enjoy passing through the clouds again as you make your way down.

As you begin to get closer to Earth, start to notice that you are going to the home, the dwelling place of your future self, yourself twenty years from now. Start to notice that the beam is taking you to meet that future self. Notice what part of the world you are in. Continue riding the beam down, enjoying the views below. Follow it all the way until it takes you to the dwelling place of your future self and drops you off right there.

Take a look around. What kind of place is this? What is it like there? What does it feel like? Look around at the outside. Then notice that there is a house, a dwelling place. Make your way toward the door. As you approach the door, see that your future self is coming to the door to warmly greet you and welcome you, and take in her presence and her face. Let her invite you inside. Notice what the inside of her house is like. Notice as she offers you something to drink and something to eat.

She brings you to one of her favorite spots in the house for a chat. She is present and ready to listen to you and share with you. Ask her what has mattered most to her over the past twenty years. She may answer you in words or just with a feeling or a facial expression or images. Listen to what she has to say.

Ask her, "What do I need to know to get from where I am to where you are? What do I need to know to get from where I am to where you are?" Listen to her answer. Again, she may answer in words, or just with a facial expression, or by giving you a certain feeling.

Ask her, "What will help me to sing my true song?" Listen to her answers. Let her answers surprise you.

Now, go ahead and ask her any other question about anything that you would like to ask her, big or small. You can ask her about a dilemma or tough situation in your life, or anything else you'd like to hear her perspective about.

Ask her, "What is your true name, other than your given name? What name are you called by?" Be open to whatever surprising name shows up first here. It may make sense to you or not.

Now, bring your visit with her to a close, knowing you can come back and visit her anytime. Thank her for the wisdom and guidance she's offered you. Notice as you are bringing your conversation to a close that she has a parting gift that she's very excited to give you, and let her bring that gift to you.

Make your way out of the house and find your way back to the beam that brought you to her. Go ahead and step on the beam and let it begin to carry you upward again. You can watch her home getting smaller and smaller beneath you, as you move through the clouds all the way up through that dark blue-black space.

Notice that next to the beam you're standing on, there's another beam, the original one that you traveled on. Step onto that beam and start to travel back down to Earth in the present time.

As you travel downward, start to see Earth coming into focus below you. See the landscape of your part of the world, your country, your region. See your city or town from a bird's-eye view. Follow that beam all the way back down into the room, where you began your journey. Slowly come back into your body. Feel your toes and your fingers, wiggle them a little bit. Feel the support of the chair or the couch beneath you. When you are ready, open your eyes and journal about what you saw, using the questions on the following page.

Postvisualization
Journaling Questions

....

Write about what you experienced during your visualization: any images, feelings, or words from your inner mentor.

What was her presence like?

What was her appearance like?

What was her home like?

What food and drink did she bring you?

Write what you can remember about her response to the specific questions you asked in the visualization:

What do I need to get from where I am to where you are?

How can I sing my true song?

Any other question you chose to ask her, and her answers.

What is your true name?

What was her parting gift to you?

More Inner Mentor Journaling Questions

In addition to answering the initial questions above immediately after you do the inner mentor visualization, you can always journal more about her. The key here, as with all the inner mentor work, is to make sure you are relaxed and open enough to actually check in with her—rather than to have your conscious mind and will supply the answers. After doing the initial visualization, many women find they can almost instantly tap into her voice. Again, some good criteria to use are (1) Did she surprise you in some way? (2) Did she offer a truly different perspective than the one you were previously operating with? If the answer to these questions is yes, you know you've tapped into her.

Here are some additional inner mentor journaling questions to explore. These are just a start. You can write about any aspect of her life that you'd like to learn more about and grow into.

What does she like to do with her free time?

What are some of her daily rituals—morning or evening routines?

How does she handle difficult relationships?

What is her relationship with money like?

What kind of art or creative pursuits does she enjoy?

How does she care for herself physically?

What does she eat, where does she eat, how does she eat?

What does she like to do to move her body, and what is her approach to exercise?

How does she take care of her health and deal with sickness or medical challenges when they arise?

How does she care for herself emotionally? What does she do with sadness? Anger? Joy?

What kind of physical environment does she create to live and work in?

TEN WAYS TO GROW
INTO YOUR INNER MENTOR

1. Sometime today, ask yourself, "What would my inner mentor do in this situation? What would she say?" Check in with her and see what the answer is. Do or say that.
2. Make some art about your inner mentor or her home. A collage, a drawing, a painting, or some photographs that evoke her—whatever your medium of choice may be.
3. Block off a window during the week to spend as she would spend it. For example, you might reserve a couple of hours on a Sunday evening to spend as she spends her Sunday evenings.

4. Think about what your inner mentor eats for breakfast, lunch, or dinner, and prepare that meal for yourself.

5. Choose a day this week to dress like your inner mentor. Wear what she would wear. See how it impacts your day and how it alters the way you see yourself.

6. When you are sitting down to write an e-mail, ask yourself, "What would she say in this e-mail?" Write *that* message!

7. Make one change to your home or office environment to make it better reflect her taste and style.

8. Bring to mind an important relationship in your life—personal or professional. How would she relate to that person? What would she say? Act as she would.

9. Identify a difficult situation or dilemma in your life and check in internally: How would your inner mentor see it? See how that shifts your perspective. If it helps, imagine walking over to her and standing side by side with her—seeing things from her vantage point, literally. How does the situation look from there?

10. Before you go into a situation, imagine you are stepping into your inner mentor's shoes, becoming her. See what she does, what she says, how she approaches it.

The Big Ideas

1. Playing big happens when we listen to the voice of the inner mentor, not the inner critic.

2. The inner mentor is an imagined version of an older, wiser you—you twenty years out into the future.

3. Once you have a vivid sense of this older, wiser, more authentic version of yourself, you'll find that she exists as a voice within you right now.

4. Your inner mentor has a very different—and very helpful—perspective on the current challenge and dilemmas you face, and you can access her for guidance.

5. Women are endlessly encouraged to seek mentors. As a counterbalance to any *external* guidance she is receiving, every woman also needs to be able to access her own inner answers, and the inner mentor is a tool for doing that.

6. Whereas many women's relationships with outer mentors involve elements of competition, times of disillusionment, and even feelings of betrayal, our inner mentors are unfailing, loving guides.

7. Your inner mentor is a North Star that can serve as your compass. She's not a destination at which you ever fully arrive.

8. Growing more and more like their inner mentors, step by step, decision by decision, allows women to play bigger in a way that is full of ease and just right for them.

9. The overarching truth that the inner mentor shows us is this: Inside, there is a voice that can remind us about our own right paths. Inside there is a voice of wisdom, calm, love, and guidance. We can turn inside for answers, again and again.

CHAPTER 3

· · ·

A Very Old New Way of Looking at Fear

A few years ago, I came across a teaching that completely changed how I understood fear. I was reading the book *Be Still and Get Going* by Rabbi Alan Lew, a brilliant writer and spiritual teacher. Rabbi Lew explained that the Hebrew Bible uses two different words for fear. The first word is *pachad*. *Pachad*, Rabbi Lew explains, is the fear of projected or imagined things, "the fear of the phantom, the fear whose object is imagined." *Pachad* is the over-reactive, irrational fear that stems from worries about what *could* happen, about the worst-case scenarios we *imagine*.

Most of us are familiar with *pachad*. It shows up as the fear that you'll horribly embarrass yourself, that the plane is about to crash, that you'll say something stupid, that *this time* the truth that you have no talent at your job will be revealed, and so on. It's what we try to help our kids move past or be brave in the face of—the fear they feel before the first day of school or when they are worried about the monster under the bed. It's the kind of fear we try to conquer in ourselves. It's the fear that often speaks through the voice of the inner critic. Thousands of years before neuroscientists discovered the overreactive nature of our fear instinct, it shows up, with its own unique term, in the Old Testament.

Here's where things get fascinating: Rabbi Lew explains that in the Hebrew Bible, there's a second word used for fear, *yirah*. *Yirah* has three different meanings:

1. It is the feeling that overcomes us when we inhabit a larger space than we are used to.
2. It is the feeling we experience when we suddenly come into possession of considerably more energy than we had before.
3. It is what we feel in the presence of the divine.

Oh. That.

When I first read about this second kind of fear, *yirah*, I thought of Mary. Mary was a corporate executive at a large regional bank and had enjoyed a long and successful career. We were working together because Mary wanted to decide what playing big would look like for her in the "encore" phase of her working life—through her sixties and beyond.

One day, in a session together, we uncovered what she *really* wanted: to move to the developing world and work for a nonprofit organization there. She wanted to do full-time the kind of service work she'd squeezed in on the side of her job for the past several decades, work she'd always loved.

As Mary finally spoke these words, her voice slowed down and sounded different—more serene, more reverent. It had a simultaneous calm and quivering to it. The space we were in seemed charged with a special kind of energy. Then Mary said, "It feels really scary to say these things. I'm terrified!"

This happened all the time in my work with women. We'd discover what they really wanted, what they felt called to do. For a moment, there would be a miraculous sense of truth and sacredness in the air. Then, the fear cloud would pass over, and they'd say something along the lines of "But I'm scared!"

I had always treated this as what, in Rabbi Lew's terms, we'd call *pachad*. I'd seen it as the regular old fear that comes up when we leave the comfort zone of the familiar and take the emotional risks that come with playing bigger. After I read about *pachad* and *yirah*, I understood I'd been missing something, something big. What Mary and others felt in those moments wasn't just *pachad*, it was also *yirah*.

Think back to the three definitions of *yirah*:

1. The feeling that overcomes us when we inhabit a larger space than we are used to
2. The feeling we experience when we suddenly come into possession of considerably more energy than we had before
3. What we feel in the presence of the divine

Mary was experiencing all these things. She was "inhabiting a larger space than she was used to" emotionally, as she stepped into this authentic dream. She was in touch with the divine—with the sacred in herself, as she articulated a longing that came from a very soulful part of her. She was suddenly in possession of more energy than she was used to, because Mary had tapped into the huge well of inner vitality and passion that we access when we go for our authentic dreams.

When we know about *pachad* and *yirah*, we can work with fear wisely, so that it doesn't hold us back from playing big. *Yirah* and *pachad* each call for very different responses in us. When we feel *yirah*, we want to simply welcome it, feel it fully, and savor it. As one graduate of the Playing Big course, Barbara Wasserman, a therapist and coach, put it, "Now, being able to differentiate between *pachad* and *yirah*, I often look for *yirah* and each day ask myself, when did I feel *yirah*? If I didn't feel it, I look for opportunities for it that I might have missed." Moving from playing small to playing big means being less and less run by *pachad* and becoming more and more comfortable living with *yirah*.

Experiences of sharing one's true voice, honoring one's soulful longings, speaking up for oneself, exposing one's creative self all bring *yirah*. Doing what your inner mentor would do also often brings *yirah*. When we label what we feel in these moments mere "fear," we can scare ourselves further, retreat, or go into a patterned reaction to fear (fight or flight). We can think we have to get away from the uncomfortable, heightened sensation of *yirah*. But if in those moments we can say, "Oh, this is *yirah*," then we can welcome the feeling as what it is: a sacred gift. We don't have to *do* anything about it. We can appreciate it, feel it. Most important, we can know it means we are connecting to the divine within and stepping into playing bigger.

When we feel *pachad*—the fear of projected or imagined things— our work is very different. *Pachad* usually leads us astray, because, by definition, it is the fear of threats that feel very real but aren't. *Pachad* fires anytime we perceive a *potential* threat to our emotional comfort zone, but the truth is we don't actually need to keep ourselves safe from every potential emotional risk. We actually need to *take* the emotional risks that come with sharing our voices and ideas more visibly and vulnerably. That's the problem with *pachad*—it fires way too frequently, often simply in an attempt to protect us from emotional risks that we don't really need (or want) to be protected from. When we feel *pachad*, we need to work on shifting away from responding out of fear so that *pachad* doesn't dictate our actions. It turns out there are lots of simple ways to do that, which we will explore in this chapter.

How to Tell the Difference between *Pachad* and *Yirah*

Of course, you can respond differently to *pachad* and *yirah* only if you know which you are feeling. How to tell the difference? For many women, both *pachad* and *yirah* bring a heightened sense of alertness, adrenaline, and a kind of "I'm-out-of-my-comfort-zone" nervous feeling. But there are subtle ways to know which you are feeling: For many women, *pachad* comes with a physical sense of contraction and tenseness, while *yirah* brings more of a spacious, fluid feeling into the body. *Pachad* is often focused on a potential future outcome; *yirah* tends to be a response to what is happening right in the present, although it certainly can come up when you are contemplating or imagining taking a step toward your playing bigger, as it did for Mary. You might associate *pachad* with your inner critic; indeed, often the critic shows up when we are feeling *pachad*. And you'll likely feel *yirah* in those moments when you are doing what your inner mentor would do. *Yirah* also includes a sense of awe. Awe has an element of fear in it—we humbly fear the greatness and grandness of what is before us—but awe encompasses much more than fear: It has elements of reverence, appreciation, and being uplifted as well.

Elizabeth, a graduate of my Playing Big course, told her young kids about these two terms for fear. Here's how they differentiated them (if they can recognize the difference, so can you):

"Today over dinner with my family I discussed *yirah* and *pachad*. My kids totally understood the two concepts and came up with examples—in fact many more than I had thought of!

"When I asked them what caused them to feel *yirah*, they said thinking about high school next year, the feeling before a basketball game (especially play-offs), thinking about a student council speech, the spring concert performance, going on a trip on a plane.

"For *pachad*, they said, 'When Huey [the nightlight] is not on, noises at night, going down the hall at night, scary rides, horror movies, sports injuries, and getting hurt.'"

As I've taught about *pachad* and *yirah* in the Playing Big course, women have shared with me how much it's helped them have a vocabulary for both concepts and to have a concept for *yirah*. Erin Geesaman Rabke explained, "It's so helpful to have that distinction between life-giving fear/awe and lizard-brain fear. I deeply relate to the quaking sort of energy that comes with inhabiting a larger space. I like renaming it *yirah* rather than fear—and now I know to follow that thread. Now, I soothe myself when the *pachad* is up and step on in when it's *yirah*."

Ana, another Playing Big course graduate, put it this way: "I didn't know to filter these intense feelings of *yirah* differently from *pachad* before. *Yirah* now strikes me as something to lean into, and I know that in the beginning it is a highly uncomfortable feeling for me."

A Deeper Way of Thinking of *Pachad* and *Yirah*

After teaching these concepts for a few years, I've come to think of them like this: We feel *pachad* when the ego perceives something it feels will *wound* the ego's fragile self-concept in some way. We feel *yirah* when the ego perceives that something has the potential to *bring us into transcendence* of the ego. Playing Big graduate Diana Tedoldi said it beautifully: "*Yirah* is the fear of dissolving a boundary, while *pachad* is the fear that I feel within that boundary."

Anytime we step into sharing our voices and into acknowledging, speaking about, or living out our authentic dreams, we move into that sacred space that transcends the ego and that the ego therefore fears. The boundaries between ourselves and others, between ourselves and the pursuit we feel passion for, begin to dissolve. This is threatening to the ego, because the ego is invested in the sense of being a separate self—separate from others, separate from nature, separate from the divine. *Yirah* is, in part, the ego's fear of its own disappearance.

How to Quiet *Pachad*

So you know what to do with *yirah*: Welcome it, savor it, allow it. What about *pachad*? How can we shift away from it and into a different state?

Typically, we are so wrapped up in the physiological experience of *pachad*—adrenaline flowing, panicky thoughts firing—that we can't see clearly what's happening. So let's take a step back now and look with an objective, learner's eye at how *pachad* operates and how it manifests, often unhelpfully, in our contemporary lives.

The human brain is hardwired to be *overreactive* to potential dangers. This functioned well for our physical survival in much earlier eras. Better for the system to trigger the fight-or-flight response and help us run away faster or defend ourselves better if there was even a *hint* of a tiger or human enemy in our midst rather than for the system to miss one of those dangers, causing us to end up, well, dead. In a context where our survival was regularly threatened, it made sense for our fight-or-flight instinct to fire in the face of any *potential* danger. It's this overreactive response to potential danger that fuels *pachad*—the fear of what *could* happen, the fear of the worst-case scenario.

In our contemporary context, the fight-or-flight response fires not just in the face of rare physical threats but also in response to any potential threats to our *emotional* safety—possible embarrassment, failure, hurt feelings. That's why, for example, standing up in front of a room to give a presentation or boldly sharing one's own original ideas can feel as scary as a physical threat: It triggers the same fight-or-flight response that was designed to help us deal with bears and avalanches. Almost comically, the most common top human fears range from fear of snakes, heights, and terrorism (things that could really kill you) to fears of public speaking and failure (things that most certainly will not kill you). We experience our fears of both emotional and physical threats with almost the same intensity.

When fight-or-flight fires in response to one of these emotional threats, it's doing a job it wasn't designed for. Adrenaline coursing through our veins doesn't help us deal with what feels emotionally scary—in fact, it makes it harder for us to cope because it interferes with our ability to think clearly. This gets in the way of our playing big because, of course, to stretch into playing bigger we need to take many emotional risks, doing things that expose us to failure, criticism, or attack.

As a good, extra-cautious protective system, the fight-or-flight response gets activated when (1) a situation that caused you hurt or pain in the past occurs again (for example, you had a traumatic performance review and now you have another review coming up), or (2) you find yourself facing something that you've previously observed causing *others* hurt or pain (for example, you watched your mom struggle because she had no financial independence and now something is coming up in your life that makes you feel at risk of losing your financial independence).

However, fight-or-flight fires when something occurs that's in some vague way similar to what's caused you hurt or pain in the past. This last piece is especially problematic and often results in our being very misled by our fears. In a 1920 study (a study that would never be permitted today), an eleven-month-old boy—Albert B.—was presented with a white rat. Initially he happily and calmly played with it, unafraid. Then experimenters conditioned little Albert to fear the white rat by making a loud noise every time they handed him the animal—startling poor Albert and making him cry. Soon, when the white rat appeared, even without the sound, Albert began to cry. He'd come to fear not just the noise but also the associated white rat. Quickly, his fear extended to *other furry objects*—a rabbit, a furry dog, and even an experimenter with a white, fluffy beard. Over the last hundred years, this kind of result has been replicated again and again (in more humane experiments), demonstrating how humans generalize from specific fears to broader ones. I'm guessing that you, like me, can recognize this pattern in your own life: Maybe you had a harsh painting teacher and then came to feel afraid of taking a painting class or art courses in general. I had so many fear-inducing experiences in P.E. as a kid that now even a game of volleyball on a family vacation freaks me out. As our fears expand to include a wide set of loosely associated things, we hold ourselves back from playing bigger.

When you feel yourself experiencing *pachad*, you'll want to immediately take some steps to shift out of it. Below you'll find fifteen simple tools for moving out of fear and into a different state of being. Some are what I call heart-based tools. These use emotions as the way in to reducing fear. Some are cognitive tools that utilize our rational thinking to help us reduce fear. Some are somatic tools, which use the body as the entry point.

There are *many* different ways to quiet fear, and I want you to be able to sample them and see what works for you. I've included fifteen of my favorites, here. You'll find that certain ones really click for you while others don't, and that different ones work for you in different kinds of situations. Try them out over time and see which ones you like best. And here's the really good news: Every one of these tools takes less than five minutes to use. You can easily integrate them into a short pause in the midst of a busy day.

Fifteen Fear Practices for *Pachad*

Heart-Based Tools

1. Tap into your inner mentor. When you feel afraid, nervous, or panicky about something, ask your inner mentor how *she* would see the situation. Bring her your fears and see how she responds.

How to do it: When you are feeling afraid, slow down for a moment, take a breath, and bring your inner mentor to mind. If the situation allows, you can close your eyes for a few moments and picture her and her home. Pay her a visit and see what she says about the thing you fear. If time and circumstances don't allow for that, simply picture her in your mind's eye and ask yourself, "What would she do in this situation?"

2. Invite love in. This is one my favorite tools. I learned it from spiritual teacher Marianne Williamson, and I use it all the time. It refers not to romantic love or interpersonal love but love as a state of consciousness, a state of being. When we invite love in, there simply isn't room for fear.

How to do it: When you feel afraid, say a little prayer or intention: "I invite love into this situation" or "I ask for help shifting out of fear and into love." Or you might say, "May I be the representative of love in this situation. May I be the embodiment of love in the room."

3. Get curious. Curiosity is a miracle drug for treating fear. Curiosity simply wants to discover what is true. That pure, childlike sense of wanting to discover and learn can't coexist with fear.

How to do it: In any situation where you feel afraid, ask yourself, "What about the situation can I become authentically curious about?" Let your curiosity lead you. When you notice fear creeping back in, go back to the question, What about this situation am I curious about? Put your focus there.

For example, let's say you feel afraid of writing your memoir, because you're worried it will be embarrassing or people won't like it. Ask yourself, what about this memoir-writing process am I truly curious about? You might find you are curious about the question, What will this writing process feel like for me? or, What will I discover when writing? You might even wonder about things you were worried about before, but *without the worried tone,* asking yourself, "Will I stick with this project, or will my interest fade? I wonder if people will be able to absorb what I'm saying, and if so, what kind of reader?"

It's impossible for pure curiosity and fear to coexist in any moment; we can be in only one state or the other. In addition to moving us out of fear, curiosity has a lot of other positive side effects: It also energizes us and brings a sense of wonder and playfulness to our work.

4. Shift into another positive state. Fear is a state of consciousness. When we consciously step into another state of consciousness, fear gets displaced. Curiosity and love (the tools above) are two such energies. What other energies displace fear for *you*? You might experiment with consciously shifting out of fear and into one of these energies/approaches/stances: joy, experimentation, adventure, authenticity, intimacy, acceptance, whimsy, humility, grace.

How to do it: Pick an energy—from the list above or one of your own—and when you feel fear, take a breath, remember that energy, and call it into your mind and heart. You can sometimes do this simply by thinking of the word and setting the intention to shift into that mode. Or look at an image that helps you connect to that energy (for example, a photo of the ocean might help you connect to a sense of calm, or a picture of your kids might inspire a sense of playfulness), or listen to a song that helps connect you to that energy. When you've tapped into the emotion, bring that to the situation you feel fearful about.

5. Reconnect to your desire to serve. Your sense of purpose is bigger than your fear. When you reconnect with your desire to serve, you can often move yourself right past your fears.

How to do it: When you are feeling afraid, remember the people you are hoping to positively impact through what you are doing. You can simply bring them to mind, write about them, or look at an image that reminds you of them.

For example, Carissa wanted to share her journey of coping with the loss of her eyesight. When she felt afraid about speaking up about it, worried that no one would care about or respond to her story, she remembered the people she wanted to serve: others who were becoming blind or who were going through other challenging illnesses. Thinking of them would pull her out of her fear and get her into action.

6. Talk with your younger self. Over the years, I've learned that each of our fears is rooted in an experience we had at a specific chronological age. Often, going back in our minds and hearts to that earlier time helps us dissolve the fear.

How to do it: When you feel afraid about something, close your eyes, take a few deep breaths, and ask yourself, "How old does this afraid part of myself feel?" You might find that the afraid part feels three, or eight, or thirteen, or twenty-five years old. Trust whatever answer intuitively pops up, whether it makes sense to you or not.

Then picture yourself at that age. Look at that young woman or girl and ask her, "What are you really afraid of here?" Listen, really listen, to what she says. Then ask her, "What do you need?" She may need reassurance of some specific kind, protection from a danger, or your help or comfort. She'll let you know. In reply, let her know you'll give her what she needs to be safe. As you do this, you are "reparenting" her—being the loving, protective adult you probably didn't have access to, in the way you needed, at this earlier age when the fear was imprinted.

You may find you need to go through several rounds of dialogue with this younger self to get to the heart of the reassurance or help she truly needs from you and for her to trust that you are really going to give it to her. When she's heard what she needed to hear, you'll know right away. You'll feel a kind of inner shift as she finds contentment and lets you know she's okay. Then you'll notice that the fear you felt before will dramatically lessen in its intensity or even dissolve entirely.

Cognitive Tools

7. Label it. When we give written or verbal labels to our emotions, simply naming what we feel, it decreases the intensity of those emotions.

How to do it: When you notice you are feeling afraid, label the feeling: "I'm afraid about *x* right now." You can speak the words out loud to someone, think them silently to yourself, or write them down.

8. Analyze truth, possibility, probability. Often, we fear a very nonspecific outcome. Get specific about the outcome you are worried about, assess the likelihood of its occurring, and check to see if you have any evidence that it's going to occur. Our highly developed analytical minds can actually help us here rather than get in our way!

How to do it: Look at what you fear and ask, How likely is it that that will occur? Do I have any evidence it will occur? For example, let's say you are preparing for an important presentation to a client, but you find yourself feeling panicked that you've totally gone the wrong direction and will lose the client entirely after this presentation. You can ask yourself, "Do I have any evidence that I've gone the wrong direction here? How likely is it—really—that they would sever our relationship based on one presentation, especially one we've done a lot of work on, like this one?"

9. Come back to the present moment. As we explored in this chapter, *pachad* fear is always related to our anticipation of possible *future* outcomes. We can return to sanity by coming home to the present moment.

How to do it: When you feel afraid about a potential future outcome, turn your attention to what is happening in the present. Notice the sights, smells, and sounds in your midst. Notice any sensations in your body. Notice your breath. When I'm afraid of a potential future outcome, I sometimes also ask myself, "Is there really any problem right now?" or, "What is the situation now?" to remind myself that the things I fear haven't happened yet and that, in the present, I'm doing okay and coping just fine with whatever is happening.

10. Follow the fear to the endgame. A few years ago, I was coaching a young woman named Radha in my Playing Big program. She wanted to start her own software-development firm but was terribly afraid of the financial risk and the potential professional failure. I asked her, "Okay, let's say the business fails—what would you do then?"

"Oh, God, I'd feel horrible. I'd feel embarrassed, like a failure, and really worried about ending up totally broke," she said.

"Okay, then what?" I asked.

"Then what? Well, I've never really thought about that before," she replied. She thought quietly for a moment. "I guess I'd move in with my older sister or parents for a bit, while I figured out what I wanted to do next and got back on my feet financially. And then, I'd find another job, back doing the kind of work I do now, probably."

As she played out this path, Radha calmed down. She could see the path she'd walk if that worst-case scenario came true, and when she actually thought through it step by step, that path wasn't actually so bad.

Fear paralyzes us by threatening the worst-case scenario outcomes, *without having us think about what we would do if that outcome occurred*. When we do imagine how we'd respond, we usually find our resilience and think of the resources available to us. We realize we'd recover. We'd be okay. This is what I call following fear through to the endgame.

How to do it: In writing or talking with a support person, ask yourself, "If the bad outcome that I fear came to pass, then what? What would I do? If I send in the application and get rejected, then what? If I hold the party and it is full of awkward moments, then what?" Keep asking the "then what?" question until you find your sense of resourcefulness and being okay with what happens.

Note: If you find that asking "then what?" over and over again puts you into panic about this thing (rather than sparking your resourcefulness), you have some deeper work to do on this fear! Check out tool #15 for this deeper work.

Somatic Tools

11. Breathe. Many kinds of deep-breathing exercises can reduce fear and help you shift into a calm, relaxed state.

How to do it: One simple way to do this is belly breathing. Place one hand on your abdomen and inhale through your nose, focusing on breathing into your belly—not your chest. Feel your belly expand outward with your inhalation. Then, exhale through pursed lips, as if you were whistling. Feel your belly contract inward toward your spine. Take it slow with your inhalation and your exhalation, giving yourself time to breathe deeply.

12. Do a physical relaxation. Releasing muscle tension and moving the body into a relaxed state will also reduce fear.

How to do it: Slowly scan your attention across your body, beginning with your feet and then moving your attention up to your ankles, your lower legs, your knees, your upper legs, your hips, through your pelvis, torso, chest, and all the way up through the crown of your head. Spend a couple of breaths on each body part, taking deep breaths and focusing on relaxing one part of your body at a time. Imagine any tension leaving that part of your body, moving out from your body like ripples moving outward from the center of a pond. Or imagine sending your breath into that part of your body, allowing the breath to open up any tight areas and dissolving any stress or tension.

13. Visualize or look at calming imagery. Imagery—real or imagined—can also activate the parasympathetic nervous system. Studies have shown, for example, that medical patients who look at calming images before a surgery experience less pain and anxiety and leave the hospital earlier. Guided imagery has been shown to reduce stress.

How to do it: Concentrate on a calming image that's in your home or visualize a favorite place in nature. Images of loved ones, beautiful objects, or serene landscapes are all good ideas. When you are feeling afraid, spend a few moments taking deep breaths and focusing your attention on the image.

14. Use music. A host of studies have shown that music can reduce anxiety, stress, and fear.

How to do it: Put on music that's calming to you and that gives you a comforting, safe feeling or a lighthearted, carefree one. Then ask yourself, what if I approached this situation I fear in the mood/attitude of this song?

15. Move through it. I know that when I go into that fight-or-flight response, I don't just want to avoid or attack the thing I fear, I want to avoid or attack the *feeling of fear* itself. I want the uncomfortable feeling of fear to go away.

There is a third way to respond to the feeling of fear—neither fight nor flight, neither trying to attack/change it nor trying to escape it, but instead being utterly present to it. It's odd but true: When we consciously and fully feel our fear, while breathing and exploring our emotions, we can move through it and do what can best be described as getting to the other side of it. We *pass through* the fear, or perhaps the fear passes through us.

This tool requires a bit more slowing down than the others, and can provoke some emotionally intense feelings along the way. It's not a tool you'd want to use for working through fears related to a major trauma, unless you have a trained support person with you. But for other kinds of fears, it works beautifully and often has long-lasting effects.

How to do it: When you are feeling afraid, notice where the physical experience of your fear manifests in your body. Does it feel like a knot in your chest, a fluttering in your stomach, or a tingly pain in your limbs? Put your attention on that place and on that physical sensation. Holding your attention there, take some long deep breaths and send the breath into that part of your body. Keep noticing your physical sensations, labeling them aloud or silently. For example, you might think to yourself, Oh, the tightness in my stomach moved lower. Now the feeling changed to more of a burning . . . , and so on. For several minutes, take conscious breaths, pay attention to the sensations in the body, and describe them to yourself.

During this time, the emotions/sensations may grow more intense. You may have the sense of descent into a darker, more difficult place. Stay with it. Keep breathing, noticing, describing the changes to yourself.

Eventually, often after the most intense moments, you'll hit the "bottom" of that descent. You'll feel a shift, which sometimes feels like an actual sense of hitting a bottom floor and then rebounding, popping up. Sometimes it feels just like a clearing or sudden change in energy. You'll find yourself on the other side of the fear. You've moved through it.

This is another one of the tools that can be difficult to do—especially for the first time—on your own. It can also feel safer to do this with a guide.

Check out the audio meditation at www.taramohr.com/pbbook materials, which will guide you through this tool.

We all need a fear tool kit, because fear will arise on the journey to playing bigger. Again and again, we'll be asked to risk failure, criticism, rejection, even ridicule as we share our voices and ideas, as we seek to change the status quo, and as we seek to change ourselves.

We'll be asked to step into greater visibility and vulnerability. We'll be required to set new boundaries in relationships, to shift power balances, to reclaim space. We'll be stretched to do things differently than we have before, to walk into the unknown. All these things evoke fear, so we need to understand how to navigate it wisely.

How Does *Pachad* Show Up in Your Life and Career?

Fear Fact	Shows Up Like This	Journaling Questions
Pachad shows up to help us recognize and react to any possible **future** dangers/hurt—physical or emotional.	"I'm afraid that if I apply for that job, I will hear back that I'm not qualified enough—and that rejection will just really sting." "I'm afraid that I'm going to screw up this presentation."	What potential future emotional dangers do you fear, especially around your playing bigger? How do these fears about the future impact the present?
Pachad causes the specific behaviors of **escape and avoidance**.	"I'm afraid I won't get the promotion, so I'm not going to apply for it." "I'm afraid of feeling clueless when meeting with that investment advisor, so I keep procrastinating on having the appointment."	What are you avoiding or escaping right now because you are afraid?
We develop many of our fears as a result of **our own painful experiences**.	"My parents always scolded me for being too argumentative and rebellious. Now when I need to speak up, I'm terrified that I'll be harshly criticized."	What painful experiences from earlier in your life taught you what to fear? What did they teach you to fear?

We also learn what to fear **by watching other people** go through fear-inducing experiences.	"Growing up, I watched my dad struggle to find work and make enough money. I became afraid of being in that position myself. A lot of my career and life decisions have been motivated by that fear."

"I remember being a teenage girl and watching Hillary Clinton be utterly tarred and feathered in the press for saying she wasn't just going to make cookies. I learned to be very afraid of saying anything too feminist." | What did you learn to fear by watching others go through fear-inducing or painful experiences? |
| Like little Albert, we **generalize** from specific fear-inducing experiences to fear a wider set of associated circumstances. | "I had a horrible performance review ten years ago—my boss was so harsh. Now I find I'm super nervous about any kind of performance review situation."

"In college, I was sexually harassed at a frat party, and now I feel afraid at parties where there are crowds of young guys." | What painful experiences have caused you to fear a wider set of similar situations? |
| We are **not too good at figuring out what to fear**. We tend to perceive threats where they do not exist and miss threats that do exist. | "I'm afraid of embarrassing myself when I'm giving a presentation—even though there is little basis for that fear. On the other hand, I never feel 'afraid' about wasting time overpreparing for those presentations—even though that's probably a much bigger threat to my career." | What kind of irrational, overreactive fears invade your consciousness?

In what ways do you fear the wrong thing—the dramatic potential disaster rather than the more boring (but more real) threat in front of you? |

Journaling Questions

....

Recall an experience of pachad. *What was it like? What triggered it?*

How do you want to respond the next time you feel pachad? *Which of the tools for quieting* pachad *might you like to try out?*

Recall an experience of yirah. *What was it like? What brought it about?*

How do you want to respond the next time you feel yirah? *What does welcoming or embracing* yirah *look like for you?*

The Big Ideas

1. In the Old Testament, there are two different words used for fear. *Pachad* is the fear of projected or imagined things. *Yirah* is the feeling that we have (1) when we suddenly come into possession of more energy than we are used to, (2) when we inhabit a larger space than we are used to, and (3) when we are in the presence of the divine.

2. For many women, playing big—whether we're just considering an action or are in the midst of one—evokes both *pachad* and *yirah*.

3. Playing big is, in part, about shifting away from *pachad* and toward *yirah*. This means when we experience *pachad* we take a moment to intentionally change our state of being. We aim to live less affectedly by our *pachad*-type fears. At the same time, we seek out and embrace experiences of *yirah*.

4. *Pachad* arises when the ego perceives something that could threaten its fragile self-concept. *Yirah* arises when we step into something—or contemplate stepping into something—that transcends the ego and moves us into the higher self.

5. Our work with *yirah* is to notice it and welcome it for what it is.

6. Our work with *pachad* is to quiet it and manage it, because *pachad*-type fear often misleads us, causing us to retreat from any emotional risk or potential harm, thereby preventing us from sharing our voices, stretching out of our comfort zones, and pursuing our dreams.

CHAPTER 4

• • •

Unhooking from Praise and Criticism

I received a lot of praise about my writing when I was growing up. I was the kid whose paper or short story or poem was read aloud by the teacher to the class. I won writing awards and heard all kinds of superlative comments from my teachers and parents.

In the very early days, that worked fine—meaning it didn't interfere with my love for writing or my ability to write. In third grade, when my best friend, Judy, and I spontaneously decided it would be fun to write a book of poetry together, we wrote playfully and with ease; it was just a nice bonus when our teachers and parents heaped praise on us. When I'd write essays or short stories for school, I loved the process, and it was just a pleasant little additional perk when a teacher liked the product.

But over time—in my teen and early adulthood years—that changed. I became so used to writing with the payoff of praise that when praise didn't come, I felt like a failure. And when criticism came? It *stung*. It made me feel unsafe, misunderstood, or like a fraud—as if my writing talent had run out or my lack of writing talent had been exposed. After receiving any kind of criticism, or even when a piece of writing didn't earn superlative praise, I felt thrown off, and I couldn't return to the desk and write comfortably again.

As I got older and more serious about writing, this became a bigger problem; I entered more critical environments—advanced writing workshops, competitive submissions processes—in which tough feedback was the norm. I became distracted by the questions: Am I really a good writer? Are they (the teacher or the other students in the workshop) going to like this? I became afraid when I sat down to write, which of course made my writing clunky and less authentic, and changed writing from a passion I found joy in to a stressful—too stressful—task.

Over time, the fear of not being good enough grew so intense that I stopped writing entirely. I call this my seven-year sabbatical from writing, sponsored by my inner critic. As the years went on, I missed writing and creative expression terribly. I wanted to go back to it, but my insecurity made the process excruciating, because my head was so full of worries about how my work would be received.

One day, toward the end of that seven-year fallow period, I was sitting in front of my computer, trying, once more, to get back into my writing routine. By this time, I knew that writing was a part of my path. I knew my inner mentor was very much a writer. I knew the work I longed to do had creativity at its center and involved expressing my ideas in the world. But I didn't know how to get my unencumbered writing life back.

Suddenly, a thought flashed in my head: "Tara, if you want to write, you've got to let go of what other people will think. You've got to give up on the 'love me, praise me' thing. You are going to have to do this in a different way than you've written in a very long time. You are going to have to write for you—for your joy, for your pleasure, for your self-expression, not for anyone else's approval."

That day, I wrote because I am a woman who loves writing. And I did something I can best describe as taking back the authority around my own work. Before that day, I thought of myself as the writer, and of *those people* out there as the judges of that writing. I suddenly saw that I could join them as a judge of my work, that I had the right—as much as they did—to look at my writing and determine what I thought was good, what needed improvement, what I was proud of.

It felt kind of like kicking people out of the immediate space around my writing, an intimate space I could suddenly see I had left way too open to the whims and sentiments of others. I began to reclaim the space around my writing for myself and to push other people's reactions to a more distant perimeter, where they couldn't quite penetrate to the heart of me.

That allowed me to write. It allowed me to press "Publish" and share my work on my blog a couple of times a week, every week, for more than five years now. It allowed me to start submitting work to popular publications. It allows me now to write this book. Most important, it opened up my creative channel again.

One other part about the move I made that day was important: I didn't ask myself to stop caring entirely what other people think. I didn't try to stop wanting praise, lots of readers, plenty of blog comments, a positive reception from the audience. I didn't give up on wanting the magic of human connection that can happen between a writer and a reader. That would have been unrealistic, and, I think, it would have denied a basic humanness in me. The desire in each of us to know we matter to others is a healthy desire. The desire to know our work is effective in doing what we intended to do is an important desire. The part of us that wants to know that we're appreciated and warmly received is a fundamental part of us, a part to be honored. But it needs to be only one part and, importantly, not the driving one.

For me, there's a certain sweetness, a pleasure, that still comes with positive feedback. The big shift was that the sweetness became like a cherry on top of an ice cream sundae—rather than being the sundae itself. Praise became a nice addition, but the work itself was where the real fulfillment came from. The work itself was the point.

This is how I think of being "unhooked" from praise and criticism. Self-expression and service become the sundaes, and praise is just a lovely cherry on top.

Getting Hooked by Praise and Criticism

My story with writing is one of the ways I got hooked by praise and criticism, how an overattachment to what others thought took me away from my own most meaningful work and greatest creative passion. What happened to me unfortunately happens for so many women. In fact, *most* of the fears that women have around playing bigger are about what other people will think: "People won't like what I have to say." "My colleagues will think I don't know what I'm talking about." "My family will disapprove." To truly play big we have to unhook from praise and criticism—to no longer depend on others' positive feedback or fear their disapproval.

Being hooked by praise and criticism takes many different forms. I think of Deb, who worked in domestic violence prevention. She'd always been a "star" in her organizations, receiving consistent positive feedback from her supervisors and peers. Her playing bigger desire was to start her own innovative domestic violence prevention program, based on what she'd learned during her twenty years working on the issue. She knew her approach would likely be controversial and draw criticism from other leaders in the field. A fear of the criticism she *might* receive kept her from launching her program. Deb had become hooked by praise and criticism in one of the ways many high-achieving women do: We don't know how to deal effectively and easefully with negative feedback, so we curtail our career ambitions to avoid receiving the worst of it.

Mimi had the opposite problem. She was raised in a family and a culture where standing out—even for positive reasons—was frowned upon. She'd come to realize she was holding herself back in her work at a large corporation because she was afraid that being too successful and receiving too much praise would cause a backlash from her peers and separate her from others. This is another, perhaps more subtle way many women get hooked by praise—they self-sabotage, never talk about their accomplishments, or conform to the levels of accomplishment of those around them in order to avoid praise.

Rachel was scarred by criticism she'd received in the past. She'd attended a prestigious fine arts graduate program where her photography was frequently critiqued by professors and visiting artists. Her art wasn't in line with what was fashionable at the time, and she was told again and again that her work was too sentimental, too idealistic, not political or weighty enough. After graduate school, that criticism kept her from producing the kind of work she most wanted to. Like Rachel, many women are hooked by criticism they received long ago.

Mandy, a tech entrepreneur, was spending hour after hour in

meetings with advisors, other entrepreneurs, and potential investors who she respected—diligently gathering their feedback on her business idea. She felt obligated to incorporate nearly everyone's feedback (after all, she had handpicked these wise people to meet with!) and to change her product again and again until it won over her critics. Doing so was slowing her down and diluting her original vision.

All these women are hooked by praise and criticism in different ways: Deb is paralyzed by fears of the criticism that might come her way if she starts to play bigger. Mimi shies away from any kind of action that might single her out for praise. Rachel isn't doing what she loves to do because she's scarred by criticism she's received in the past. Mandy is stalled because she is trying to please everyone and to incorporate too many people's feedback in her work.

Playing big is a kind of bold and free motion, and both the fear of criticism and seeking of praise limit that movement. When we are petrified of criticism or are in need of constant approval, we simply can't play big. We can't innovate, share controversial ideas, or pursue our unique paths. In this chapter, you'll look at exactly how and where dependence on praise or avoidance of criticism is hampering *your* playing big. You'll also learn how to work with feedback, both positive and negative, so that it helps you and doesn't hold you back. This is essential because any kind of playing big will bring both praise and criticism. We need to know how to respond to both in ways that propel us forward.

While I call this work *unhooking* from praise and criticism, it's not about your becoming impervious to others' reactions. It is about your becoming less hindered by those reactions. It's about how you can learn to savor praise but not depend on it or be driven by it. It's about how you can learn to incorporate criticism when it is useful, but not be immobilized by it.

Six Reasons We Care So Much
About What Other People Think

When I first created the Playing Big course, I knew this topic had to be a part of it, because I'd seen how difficulties with both praise and criticism had held back friends and colleagues, my coaching clients, and myself. As I showed women the initial course syllabus, they'd often point to the words "Unhooking from Praise and Criticism" and say, "Oh, yes, I need *that*! I know I need a thicker skin, but I don't know how to get it."

Yet when I started teaching this topic, I noticed something. When we'd get to this module and begin talking about our attachment to praise or our fears of criticism, voices would quiver. There was a lot of fear and intense emotion. The way women were talking

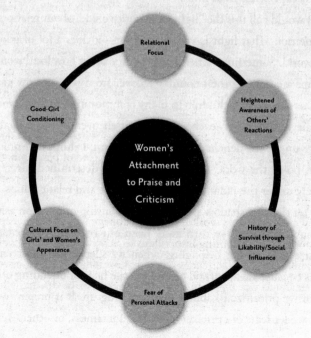

about their fears of criticism and need for approval felt life-and-death serious, like a matter of survival.

I got curious about that. Why does what others think about us feel so scary, so loaded? Why does praise feel like a lifeline? Why does this issue get us at our very cores?

I think there are a number of reasons, and they compound one another. When we understand them, we can see why this topic runs so deep for us.

1. Relational focus. Whether by nature or nurture or both, many women are very relationship-oriented. We care for and nurture other people. We take others' perspectives into account. We do what we can to preserve harmony and connection in our families, communities, and teams at work. We want to be kind and to know that others experience us as kind.

I would call this the "light," the positive side, of our relationship orientation. That light is very important—it does a lot of good in the world. Sometimes, when I read a story about how local women's groups are helping their country recover from war, or how grandmothers are raising children in many communities, or how a mostly female workforce of teachers extends itself over and over again to make up for the deficits in our school system, I think that much of what holds the world together is women's determined, fierce, yet largely under-the-radar sustaining of people and relationships.

Yet there's a shadow side to our relationship orientation as well. It shows up when we turn away from our own truths because of outsize fears of not belonging, when we silence our most radical ideas because we are afraid of rocking the boat or offending others, when we prioritize likability over speaking up. It is present whenever we let fears of criticism, rejection, loneliness, or others' resentment stand in the way of our playing bigger, growing into our inner mentors, or sharing our ideas. Our relationship orientation is a part of what makes us particularly wounded by criticism and particularly seeking of praise and approval from others.

2. Heightened awareness of others' reactions. I call this "the noisy room." I feel as if all my life, I've been walking into noisy rooms—rooms filled with information about the moods, shifting attitudes, and interpersonal dynamics of the people present. Of course, most of that "noise" is silent—it's expressed in body language, facial expressions, subtle cues from people in the room. But all that information creates a lot of noise in *my head*.

Even as a kid, I knew this was both a good thing and a problem. On the playground, I could quickly figure out which kids were influential, how the social groups were composed, and what I needed to do and say to fit in. But I could also see how that caused me to hang back from jumping on the swings or joining the kickball game right away, just me being me. Instead, I was watching all the social cues so I'd know how to change myself to fit in best. My focus was out there, and I was a chameleon. Sometimes I envied the kids who just seemed to pounce into the action, loud and free and themselves, oblivious to the dynamics around them. They were shaping the landscape, not adapting to it.

When I entered the work world, many of the professional meeting rooms I sat in felt incredibly "noisy" to me too. I'd pick up on who was engaged and who was disengaged, who seemed threatened by what was going on, who had more power and who less. I noticed all kinds of subtle cues—body language, tones of voice. It was sometimes strategically useful to have all that information, but just as often, it could be distracting.

A host of studies have found that as a group, women are more skilled than men at reading other people's facial expressions and body language. That means women literally *get more information* about other people's thoughts and feelings than do our male counterparts. And, the research has shown, this information isn't always helpful. In a study conducted at Harvard University, social psychologists Hillary Elfenbein and Nalini Ambady found that individuals with high emotional recognition abilities frequently read hidden negative expressions from their colleagues. This "emotional eavesdropping" turned out to be useful in some workplace situations but *harmful* in others, where it was found to be distracting and upsetting, and where it lowered overall productivity. The researchers conclude, "People may have problems not only when they are unable to read the social cues around them, but also when they have the potential to 'read too much' in a particular situation . . . reading negative expressions that were unintended or uncontrollable can be unproductive for individuals because it can provide harmful information easily blown out of proportion. . . ."

If a person with very high emotional intelligence is giving a pitch to investors, for example, she may pick up on ten people's moods within the first few minutes. That information can be an advantage. If she can detect that a key person in the room seems uninterested in her pitch and needs to be won over, she can act on that information, trying a new approach she thinks might resonate more with the investor or following up specifically with that individual to see if there are questions or concerns she can address. But her keen sensitivity to what's happening in the room might be more a liability than an asset. If she feels anxious about subtly antagonistic facial expressions she's noticed, her worry may affect her performance. She may become focused on trying to dissuade the one reluctant listener in the corner, when that guy's opinion doesn't actually matter. She may think that the negative body language she sees indicates that her pitch isn't going well, and she may get distracted by trying to change course, when in fact she's doing just fine and the nonverbal cues in the room have nothing to do with her.

If someone with *low* emotional intelligence gives a pitch to a group of investors, by contrast, he may miss cues in the room about who is engaged, who is getting bored, who's offended. While he doesn't have access to that potentially useful information, his "deafness" to those cues also leaves him free to focus on saying what he came there to say. That often works out really well—by the time his pitch is over, maybe disengaged listeners are engaged, maybe their reaction didn't matter anyway, or maybe whatever was happening in the room had to do with the previous topic at the meeting, and not with him.

Women's ability to pick up on others' nonverbal cues and adapt when necessary can be a strength. Yet all that noise, all that information about what's going on for others, can make it hard to hear and stay true to our own voices.

3. A history of survival through likability and social influence.

For most of history, likability and others' approval was women's lifeline. We couldn't protect our own safety through physical, legal, or financial means. We couldn't defend ourselves through a kick or a punch, nor could we rely on the law if our safety was threatened. We couldn't use a dollar of our own to get out of town or support ourselves independently if we needed to, because we couldn't hold property in our own names. *For millennia, we could ensure our survival by complying with what was approved of or desired by those with greater power.* Being likable, or at least acceptable, to stronger, more powerful people was a survival strategy. This is part of why disapproval feels so unsafe to many women: For millennia, *it was life threatening*. And it is still life threatening to women who live under oppressive regimes or in violent homes. Knowing that impacts our psyches, consciously and unconsciously. When a woman is trying to unhook from dependence on praise, it's no trivial matter. She is working on retraining her mind from generations-old conditioning about what is required to *survive*.

4. Fear of personal attacks. I can remember many times in my life when I've watched women be viciously and personally attacked for speaking out. Hillary Clinton advocating for health care. Sheryl Sandberg for encouraging women to lean in. Reporter Christiane Amanpour for expressing even a hint of anger about the deaths of children in Syria. Worst of all, we see women attacking other women in this way, and we even participate in those attacks, reinforcing what's not allowed—in us or other women. This is one of the reasons we can become so afraid of criticism: Often, when it comes to powerful women, it is vulgar, shaming, and inappropriately personal. When hostile attacks about these women are broadcast across our media, I always wonder, What is this teaching women about what will happen to them if they speak out? What is this imprinting on my psyche about what will happen to me if I speak out? How might what I've seen happen to other women heighten my fears about the criticism that will come my way if I play bigger?

5. Cultural focus on girls' and women's appearances. Girls grow up learning that how they look is extremely important. Movies, TV shows, toys, video games, and, of course, ubiquitous advertising tell the same story again and again: A woman's destiny has everything to do with how attractive she is—especially in men's eyes. This sends women a larger message about the importance of *how we are perceived by others*. While the explicit message women receive is, "Be beautiful, be thin, be attractive; that's what matters," what this says to us at a deeper level is that *how others perceive us* is what matters. That how you are seen from the outside matters more than what you experience on the inside. No wonder we develop the idea that the praise and criticism we receive from others is extremely important.

6. Good-girl conditioning. Last but not least, and perhaps most obviously, there is our good-girl conditioning: Be nice. Be considerate of others. Don't rock the boat. Be likable. Be modest and solicitous at all costs. Don't ever be angry, aggressive, or arrogant. In the context of this conditioning, the withdrawal of others' praise or their negative reactions to us feel particularly transgressive and scary.

Five Principles for Unhooking from Praise and Criticism

So, what to do about our patterns of getting hooked? Let's talk about five principles that help us unhook from praise and criticism:

> **Principle 1:** Feedback Doesn't Tell You about You; It Tells You about the Person Giving the Feedback

Most of us walk through life thinking that feedback gives us information about *ourselves*—our abilities, strengths, and weaknesses, our performance. I invite you to consider a radical, new idea: Feedback doesn't tell you anything about you; it tells you only about the person giving the feedback.

If you show your paintings to three successful artists in your community, and none of them like your work much, does that give you any *facts* about the quality of your artwork? No—it only gives you facts about what those three people like or don't like. What if a million people don't like your paintings? Surely that tells you that you aren't a "good artist," right? I'd argue it doesn't. Rather it tells you something about what *contemporary viewers* dislike.

If you pitch your business idea to a potential investor and that investor isn't interested, that tells you something about what gets her attention and what doesn't. It does not actually tell you anything about your merit as an entrepreneur or the quality of your idea. If your relatives think you're an irresponsible mom, that doesn't tell you about your mothering. It tells you something about what they see as responsible parenting.

Feedback gives us facts about the opinions and preferences of those giving the feedback. It can't tell you about your merit or worthiness. When we understand this, we're free; we're free to seek, gather, and incorporate feedback.

Because here's the thing: Feedback is wildly important. Stay with me for part two of the idea here, because part two is very important: Feedback shouldn't be dismissed because it doesn't tell you anything about you. Feedback is vital not because it tells us about our own value *but because it tells us whether we are reaching the people we need to reach.*

If an entrepreneur wants her pitch to be effective with venture investors, she *needs* to hear their feedback in order to learn what inspires them to invest. If an aspiring memoirist wants her work to be read widely, she needs to hear feedback from her intended audience. If a teacher wants her students to learn a lot and enjoy her class, she needs to know—from their feedback—whether that's happening.

When you look at feedback this way, you can approach it with a kind of exquisite calm and centeredness because you know it's just useful data, nothing more. Feedback is not meant to give you self-esteem boosts or wounds. That's not its place. It is meant to give you *tactical information* about how to reach the people you want to reach. Feedback is emotionally neutral information that tells you what resonates for your desired audience, what engages the people you want to engage, what influences the people you want to influence.

When I write a blog post, and no one comments on it, shares it on social media, or writes to me about it, I could conclude that I wrote a "bad post" and start listening to inner critic tapes that I'm not good at what I do. That would be the old paradigm: thinking the feedback tells me about me. In the new paradigm, I can see that the feedback tells me *about my readers*—about what makes a post compelling for them. The first line of thinking sends me into an unhelpful, self-obsessive, negative spiral. The second helps me rapidly improve my craft.

Think of Rachel, the photographer I talked about at the beginning of the chapter, who felt so traumatized by the rough criticism she'd received on her work in grad school. What if she were able to reframe her professors' harsh criticisms not as definitive statements of her work's merit but rather as reflections of the preferences of the school's faculty at the time? She might have quickly realized that elite academia was not where her photography was going to find its most enthusiastic viewers, but that women consumers might respond very differently. It would have been much easier for Rachel to keep taking pictures, doing what she loved to do and what she was quite talented at.

As Meeta Kaur, a writer, speaker, and the creator of a collection of Sikh American women's writings, puts it, "Now I see criticism as a source of information, somewhat akin to a news article or opinion editorial. Shifting to it being a source of information takes the sting out of it, takes the personal side out of it, and makes it useful and eye-opening."

Principle 2: Incorporate Feedback That's Strategically Useful, and Let the Rest Go

Most brilliant women love the part of any process when we gather input from others and seek their advice. It makes us feel collaborative, in relationship, humble. And we feel safe: Gathering others' opinions helps us confirm that our ideas are understandable and received well—or helps us learn if they are not. Yet we usually aren't so good at *filtering* feedback—discerning which types of feedback are critical to incorporate and which aren't.

When I went into the work world, I began noticing that many of the most effective leaders and most recognized luminaries in my field would receive lots of thoughtful feedback and criticism on their plans, but often, they'd prioritize speed, moving ahead, or just making their lives easier by not incorporating the feedback. It shocked me at first, because it was so different from the way most women I knew operated. But often it turned out to be very effective: The plans or work products those leaders had were good enough without the changes others recommended—good enough both to achieve the aims of the specific project and to significantly advance their careers.

Much of the feedback you'll receive is not important to integrate into your work. This is especially true for women innovators, change agents, and activists. Some of it is plain old backlash. Some reflects people's being threatened by or not understanding cutting-edge ideas. Some reflects attachment to the old way. Some simply reflects a natural range of responses to your work. The key here is to always be asking, What feedback do I need to incorporate *in order to be effective in reaching my aims?* And what feedback really won't impact my effectiveness and is okay to ignore?

For Sevra, this was a hard-won lesson. Sevra had worked in urban planning for almost a decade. After working on several successful projects, she had an idea for a new way to organize community development projects—an approach that she felt would be more efficient and better serve all the stakeholders involved. She wanted to try it out, either within her existing company or maybe by starting a firm of her own. So she did what was natural to her: She started gathering feedback on this new approach. She talked to colleagues over lunch about it—some were enthusiastic, some less so. She called up two mentors and talked to them about it. One was supportive. The other told her it could never work unless it was done in a very different way from the one Sevra had been imagining. That mentor seemed personally threatened or upset somehow—and made a comment about how the techniques that had been carefully developed over the past fifty years couldn't just be cast aside. Then Sevra called up a couple of favorite classmates from her grad school program, people whose opinions she'd always respected. They each had a set of suggestions about how she could improve the idea. At the end of all those phone calls and coffee dates, Sevra had a wealth of feedback, much of it conflicting.

The next step for Sevra was using this principle: applying the feedback that was strategically useful and letting the rest go. First, that meant discerning which pieces of feedback she felt truly enriched her idea in an important way. Second, it meant asking, Whose feedback is important to incorporate because I need that stakeholder on board? With that question in mind, she realized she didn't need to incorporate her grad school classmate feedback. She didn't need to incorporate all the ideas from colleagues at work. But if she wanted to launch the idea within her company, she would need to address the feedback from her boss, from some of her influential coworkers, and probably from one or two mentors who were leaders in the field and whose backing would be critical.

Here's whose feedback we often *don't* need in order to effectively achieve our aims:

- **Family and friends.** Of course, it's nourishing and comforting to talk things over with family and friends whose insights you respect and whose encouragement you value. But often we turn to them for information they can't really give us. Can your best friend at work really tell you whether the career change you are contemplating is feasible? Can your dad really discern whether your business idea is promising? When you talk to them, you'll hear some mix of personal opinions on the topic, their fears, and their attempts to support you in the best way they know how—which may be thinking you need to play it safe. What you probably won't learn from them is information that will help you answer the key questions about your new project: Does it resonate with its intended audience? Are the stakeholders that need to be on board on board?

- **Mentors and experts.** Women often look for permission and validation from mentors and experts—from the mamas and papas of their fields, so to speak. You start a blog about gardening and then ask a more successful gardening blogger in your field for feedback. You have a new idea for a service your company could offer to clients, and you ask your boss whether she thinks the clients would like it. Often, though, the mamas and papas of the field won't totally get what you are proposing, may feel threatened by it and lash out, and/or can't put themselves in the shoes of your target audience.

The most important people to gather feedback from are the **intended audiences** and **decision makers** you need to influence or reach. The most important person from whom to get feedback on that gardening blog is your target reader. The most important feedback on that new service idea comes from the clients the service is intended for—only *they* can tell you whether the service is desirable or not. If you are contemplating a career move into a new industry, a recruiter or hiring manager in that field will be better able to help you evaluate the move than a friend or family member.

Ask yourself, Who am I trying to influence or engage? *That's* who you want to get feedback from. For a business, the answer to that question might include multiple stakeholders: investors, customers, potential partners. For a social-purpose organization, it might include donors and clients. For an artistic product, the answer is the potential audience.

Principle 3: Women Who Play Big Get Criticized. Period.

Sometimes, we can't see the water we're swimming in. It took me a long time to realize I held a problematic, untrue belief about criticism: that if I received it, it meant I had done something wrong. It meant I had made a mistake. Or it meant I had failed to anticipate others' reactions and adapt accordingly. Or it meant I had brought the wrong "energy" to the situation or didn't listen to my intuition enough ("spiritual" versions of "I made a mistake").

It took me quite some time to grasp that when I am playing big, criticism comes my way. There's nothing I can do to avoid that happening and often nothing I need to do about it. One of the most important mental shifts a woman can make to support her playing big is to stop thinking of criticism as a signal of a problem and to start thinking of criticism as part and parcel of doing important work.

Think of the women you admire because of the significant impact they've made on their communities, their companies, or their industries. Were they universally adored? No, to say the least. Women doing or saying anything of substance draw both criticism and praise. Some people give them a standing ovation and some throw tomatoes.

I think every woman can benefit from an "unhooked-from-criticism" role model—a woman whom she admires, whose work provokes significant criticism, and who has persevered in the face of that criticism. Your "unhooked-from-criticism" role model might be someone you know personally, a leader in your workplace, or a figure from contemporary political or public life. She might be a figure from an earlier era, or maybe your inner mentor plays this role for you. When you get tough criticism or feel afraid of criticism that *might* come your way, ask yourself, How would she handle it? What would she do in response to this? Those answers will provide you with some new possibilities for how you might proceed.

To really bring home this idea for yourself, visit a website with book reviews and look up the reviews of one of your favorite woman authors. Read several of the most positive reviews. Then read several of the most negative reviews. Do this with another favorite author, then another. The polarization and diametrically opposed opinions ("I love the characters and felt like they were real people!"/ "Her characters are so unrealistic!" or "I couldn't put it down!"/"I couldn't get interested.") become almost humorous. Reading a handful of reviews, it becomes obvious that any substantive work draws a wide range of reactions. If the authors and thinkers you most admire are getting tough criticism, you can probably expect to receive some too.

Principle 4: Criticism Hurts When It Mirrors What We Believe about Ourselves

One day, I thought back to my own most painful and paralyzing experiences of criticism: the time a teacher said my writing was stilted and awkward, and when a boy at school made a mean comment about my skinny legs and big belly, the time a teenage boyfriend made fun of the dark hair on my body, and when a famous writer said my work just "didn't go anywhere." I noticed something odd: *All* my most excruciating experiences of criticism clustered around my writing and my body.

I tried to remember, What kinds of criticism *hadn't* stayed with me? Those experiences had faded so far out of memory I had to dig them up into consciousness, but they were there: the time a boss had said I was disorganized and sloppy in my work, the time in high school some girls called me selfish and mean. Even at the time those experiences occurred, the criticism had bounced right off, as if those arrows had nowhere in me to land.

Criticisms about my writing and my body hurt so much, I realized, because they echoed what I felt about myself: *I* had tremendous doubts about my ability as a writer, and *I'd* always felt there was something wrong with my body, something to be ashamed of. The experiences of being called selfish, mean, sloppy, and disorganized didn't hurt because I felt sure, in my own heart, that I wasn't those things.

As I began to talk with women about their experiences of criticism, I found that each woman could recall incidents of criticism that hadn't upset her and that she never took personally. Each could also identify other types of criticism that crushed her and made a permanent mark on her sense of self.

The difference lay in what they believed. If the criticism aligned with a belief they held about themselves, it hurt like hell and stopped them in their tracks. But if they believed something different about themselves, they could simply ignore the feedback or, when appropriate, incorporate what was useful about it and move on. I call this the "matchup"—the symmetry between the criticism that hooks us most and the negative beliefs we hold about ourselves.

Since the criticism that most hurts us mirrors a negative belief we hold about ourselves, **often what feels like a problem with painful criticism is really a problem with what we believe about ourselves.** We're upset not because so-and-so said what they said but because their saying it catalyzed us to more acutely feel the pain of what we believe—or fear—about ourselves.

Remember Deb, the woman who wanted to start her own innovative domestic violence prevention program but was petrified of the criticism that might come her way if she did? Deb realized the criticism she most feared—leaders in her field saying she didn't have adequate expertise to start a program—reflected her own inner critic narratives: She had a voice in her own head saying the same thing. She began to use the tools for quieting the inner critic. She called on her inner mentor to get an alternative perspective, and in her inner mentor's response, she found calm reassurance that her program drew on lessons she'd learned and thoughtful reflection. As Deb began believing more and more in her own qualifications, her fear of being criticized started to fade.

Once we know that the "ouches" of criticism are mostly not about the external event, but about our internal reality, we've got power. We can utilize painful experiences of criticism to discover the negative beliefs we hold about ourselves. We can turn our focus away from the other person, away from the incident, and look inside to see what beliefs we hold that made the criticism so wounding.

Finding the Matchup with Praise

Just as we looked for the matchup with criticism, we can look for the matchup with praise. The praise we seek reflects what we most want to confirm about ourselves. For example, if we don't believe we're smart, we might strive and strive to get praise around our intelligence. If we don't believe we're attractive, we may do all kinds of things to hear "feedback" from the world that we are. This is a failing strategy. We look to external praise to confirm that we are x or y, but usually *until* we believe it ourselves, we can't believe it when we hear it from others.

Maggie, a graphic designer, found that she was constantly craving positive feedback. When she produced a new piece of work, she wanted to know—right away—that the client loved it or that her boss thought it was fabulous. She anxiously awaited their responses, felt upset when her work wasn't met with universal praise, and spent excessive amounts of time posting her work to social media sites and compulsively checking to see how much attention it had received. Maggie started to see that this stemmed from her own insecurity about her abilities. So when she found herself reaching outward for praise, Maggie started to turn the focus inward to deal with the insecurities or fears at work in those moments. She used the tools for quieting the inner critic. She reminded herself that feedback couldn't tell her if she was talented or not—it just told her if her work happened to align with her clients' or boss's expectations. Over the next couple of months, that inner work allowed Maggie to stop spending so much time and energy in praise-seeking. She could focus more on her designs and use feedback strategically—to better meet clients' expectations—rather than receive it as an emotional boost or wound. From there, she could take greater risks with her designs, which, ironically, led to much more praise from her customers and colleagues.

For me, there were years of having a kind of hole in my heart about my writing. Despite how much I sought it, any praise I received about my writing didn't stick; it passed right through that hole. Each shot of positive feedback—no matter how superlative or significant—produced only a very temporary high that then faded as I settled back into an inner critic–ridden narrative about my work.

When I came to believe my work was worthy of being written, whether others liked it or not, that changed. I had filled the inner void, and the praise I received had a solid place to land, to be planted. Instead of passing through me, it took root. I could hear and see that my work was touching people. The praise wasn't that important, because my focus had shifted to my own creative process, but I could enjoy knowing my writing was reaching and making a difference for others.

Principle 5: Ask, What's More Important to Me Than Praise?

The final principle for unhooking from praise and criticism is about remembering your true priorities. It centers on asking yourself a simple question: What is more important to me than praise or being liked in this situation? Here's what a few women had to say in answer to that question:

Being useful. Being compassionate. Being truthful. Living in my own skin fully. Inspiring others. Being true to myself. Bringing new ideas to reality. Liking myself. Being known—all of me, good and bad. My peace of mind. Getting my message out. Proving it can be done. Dignity. Making real contributions. Helping those I work with suffer less. Being effective. Acting with integrity. Doing something I believe in.

For many women, both service and self-expression are more important than praise. Rachel was able to return to her photography work by refocusing on the joy it brought her but also by thinking about the people she hoped to uplift through her work. When she thought of them, she wanted to get her pictures out there, no matter what her graduate school professors thought of them. When Deb thought about the women whom a new domestic violence program could help, she found the motivation to move forward, despite her fears of how colleagues might respond to her controversial approach.

What are your answers to the question, What's more important to me than praise?

Unhooking from Praise and Criticism

Hooked	Unhooked
I look to feedback to tell me about my talent, my merit, or the worthiness of my ideas.	I look to feedback to give me emotionally neutral, strategic information about how to most effectively achieve my aims.
I assume that feedback tells me something about me.	I know that feedback can tell me only about the people giving the feedback.
I seek feedback on my work and ideas widely—from whomever I think might have something smart to say, from the people I love and trust, from mentors and experts in the field.	I seek support from friends and family and gather feedback from a thoughtfully chosen set of people I need to influence and reach in my work: key stakeholders, decision makers, or my intended audience or customers.
I see criticism as a problem, a sign I did something wrong, or as a failure to anticipate others' reactions.	I see criticism as something that simply comes with playing big and with doing important work.
I know that some kinds of criticism hurt me terribly, and I do my best to avoid those.	I know that the criticism that hurts me most hurts because it echoes what I believe about myself, and I use painful experiences of receiving that kind of criticism as opportunities to look at and change my own beliefs.
Praise is the sundae.	My own fulfillment, service to others, and self-expression is the sundae, and praise is a lovely cherry on top.

THE PRACTICES: SIX THINGS TO DO
WHEN YOU ARE GETTING HOOKED
BY CRITICISM OR PRAISE
. . . .

1. When you receive feedback—negative or positive—remember that the feedback doesn't tell you about you, it tells you about the people giving the feedback. Ask yourself, What does this tell me about the people giving the feedback? What—if anything—does this tell me about the preferences or priorities of the people I'm trying to reach? What can this teach me about how to do my work most effectively?

2. Discern whose feedback you need to incorporate for strategic reasons, in order to reach the people you want to reach, and remember it's okay to ignore other feedback.

3. Ask yourself, What would my "unhooked-from-praise-and-criticism" role model do?

4. When criticism really stings, or when you strongly fear a certain type of criticism, look at how that criticism mirrors a belief you hold about yourself, and work on updating that belief.

5. When you find that seeking a certain kind of praise is driving you, look inward to see how that praise relates to a doubt you have about yourself, and work on addressing that inner doubt rather than seeking external validation in an attempt to resolve it.

6. Ask yourself, What's more important to me than praise or being liked here?

Journaling Questions

How have one or more of these factors impacted your relationship to praise and criticism?

- *Being relationship-oriented and prioritizing others' feelings over your own*
- *"The noisy room"—getting lots of (sometimes distracting) information about everyone else's feelings and reactions*
- *Women's history of needing to be likable and approved of in order to survive*
- *Watching other women—in your family, local community, or the media—be viciously criticized when they speak up*
- *The sense that how you are perceived is more important than what you experience from the inside out*
- *Good-girl conditioning from family, school, community, or society at large—encouraging you to always be nice and not rock the boat*

Feedback Doesn't Tell You about You; It Tells You about the Person Giving the Feedback

Recall an experience of getting tough or negative feedback. What might this tell you about the person giving the feedback rather than about you? What does it tell you about what you need to do to do your work effectively?

Recall an experience of positive feedback—something that made you feel wonderful about yourself or your work. What might this tell you about the person giving the positive feedback rather than about you?

Incorporate Feedback That's Strategically Useful, and Let the Rest Go

For one of your current projects, identify the following: Who are the people I need to influence or reach in order for this to be successful? These are the critical people from whom to gather feedback.

Is there any advice you've recently received about your work that is potentially useful, but not crucial, and that you can simply ignore rather than take time to incorporate? What feels freeing or appealing about that?

Criticism Comes with Playing Big

In this chapter we explored the idea that criticism is something that comes with doing important pioneering work. How does this idea depart from or reinforce ideas you were raised with?

Who are your "unhooked-from-criticism" role models—women whose work or words draw significant criticism but who have persevered in the face of that criticism in a way that you admire? These might be women from your personal life, your workplace, contemporary political or public life, or earlier historical eras. Or yours might be your inner mentor. If you can't think of a role model for this, pay attention as you move through your life and read the news over the next couple of weeks—you'll find her.

Imagine that this woman—your role model—is facing the criticism you are getting or that you fear. Ask yourself, How would she handle it? What would she do in response? What would she say? Let those answers provide you with some new ideas for how you can respond.

Visit a website with book reviews and go to the reviews of one of your favorite woman authors. Read several of the five-star reviews. Now read several of the one-star reviews. Write down some of your favorite contrasting statements from the reviews here. For example, you might include a line from a five-star review that extols the amazing, realistic characters in the novel, and the opposite sentiment from a one-star review—a line about how poorly developed the characters are. Then look over your notes—what did you learn? What looks or feels different around criticism in your own life and work?

Finding the Matchup with Criticism

Think about your most painful experiences of criticism. What was the criticism you received or the thing that happened to you that felt like criticism?

How does this criticism touch on a negative belief you hold about yourself? Or how does it touch on something you fear might be true about yourself?

When is the first time you can remember believing that thing about yourself? What early experiences or messages might have led to that belief?

What new self-concept would you like to replace it with?

Finding the Matchup with Praise
What is one of the kinds of praise that is most important to you?

How does that relate to a deep-down doubt you have about yourself or lessons you learned long ago about what qualities you must possess or what qualities determine your worthiness?

What Is More Important Than Praise?
What is more important to you than praise or being liked?

The Big Ideas

1. When we are dependent on praise or avoidant of criticism, we can't share controversial ideas, deal with the resistance that comes up when we are acting as change agents, or pursue our unique paths to personal fulfillment, paths that others might not understand or applaud. Becoming unhooked from praise and criticism is one of the major shifts we must make in order to play bigger.

2. A number of factors cause us to get hooked by criticism and praise: good-girl conditioning, the cultural focus on how women are perceived from the outside, women's heightened ability to read others' reactions, our relationship orientation, the unfair and hostile personal attacks women in leadership are often subject to, and a history of women ensuring their survival through likability and others' approval, in the absence of financial or legal power.

3. Some key ideas can help us unhook from criticism. The first is that feedback tells you about the person giving the feedback; it doesn't tell you about you. Whenever you are receiving feedback, you can ask, What does this tell me about the people giving the feedback? From your answer, you can learn something about the audiences you are trying to influence and reach.

4. Women who play big receive criticism. Learning to see criticism as part and parcel of doing substantive work—rather than seeing it as a sign of failing—is a critical rite of passage on the journey to playing bigger.

5. The criticism that most hurts us mirrors a negative belief we hold about ourselves. The praise we most fervently seek reflects what we most want to confirm about ourselves. What *looks* like a problem with criticism or praise is usually really a problem with what we believe about ourselves.

CHAPTER 5

• • •

Leaving Good-Student Habits Behind

We're becoming the educated class—women are, that is. Women earn 60 percent of the master's degrees in the United States, and the numbers are comparable in Europe and other parts of the industrialized West. The US Department of Education predicts that by 2021 women will represent 59 percent of all higher education students, outnumbering men in undergraduate programs as well as postsecondary education programs.

Girls are also doing better than boys in school. National reading tests indicate that as early as fourth grade, girls are performing at or above proficiency level at a much higher percentage than their male peers. Girls graduate high school with an average GPA of 3.10 as compared to boys' average of 2.90. There's even a movement of programs, scholarships, and interventions to help boys catch up.

Given all this, it seems that if there's one thing we can celebrate about women's advancement, it's our access to and performance in educational environments. But after years of working with educated women to help them play bigger, I think we need to take a closer look and ask, What are girls and women actually learning from school? Not the facts memorized or the academic skills mastered but the deeper learning, the lessons slowly absorbed, day by day, from the culture of school itself. What do nearly twenty years of school teach girls and young women about the definition of achievement? What do girls learn about what earns rewards and what doesn't, and how does that shape the adult women they become? *Most important, when we say girls are succeeding in school, what exactly are they succeeding at?*

I began thinking about these questions, because all my life I'd been a good student: working hard, earning A's, feeling proud of my good grades, and heading off to a prestigious college and graduate school. Yet in my career, I started noticing that in some ways, the skills I learned in school—the skills I thought were the ingredients for accomplishment—weren't serving me so well in the work world. In fact, they were hindering me. As I talked with other women, I saw that they too were applying their familiar "good student" work habits to their careers, but those habits sometimes kept them playing small. Blazing a bright trail in their careers—moving from "good worker bee" to "mover and shaker"—required an entirely different set of muscles, skills, and ways of being than the ones they honed in school.

I began to wonder, What if girls are doing so well in school because school requires many of the same abilities and behaviors as being a "good girl": respect for and obedience to authority, careful rule-following, people-pleasing, and succeeding in an externally imposed framework? What if women are earning more advanced degrees in part because it's harder for them to ever feel as if they've gotten enough training to start leading? And what if because of the nature of school—the skills we develop there but also the abilities we lose—all that academic training translates into their success at midlevels in organizations, but it will not translate to their increased numbers as senior leaders, change makers, and innovators?

In this chapter, we'll explore four core behaviors we learn in school that keep us playing small and the corresponding new ways of working that free us up to play bigger.

This shift may feel especially pertinent to you if you were a good-student type and high academic achiever, but it is relevant for all women, because we all spent many years being conditioned by the norms and routines of school.

Of course, the norms and routines explored in this chapter are those of the *typical* classroom. There are many burgeoning programs and innovations that offer students something different—for example, teaching interpersonal competencies and training students in leadership skills. Yet most women in the working world today were shaped by the more traditional school environment discussed here and, as a result, have some unlearning to do.

1. Adapting To versus Challenging and Influencing Authority

In school, students must *figure out what each new authority figure (the teacher) wants and then shape their work accordingly*. Teachers specify their unique requirements for everything from how a student writes her name on an assignment to how she should structure a paper to—in the early years—how she enters the classroom and organizes her possessions at her desk. Of course, these rules have a practical benefit, but the underlying skill they teach students is how to adapt to what an authority figure wants, and the underlying lesson they teach is that success depends on that adaptation. In elementary school, this means students mold themselves to a new set of requirements annually, with each new teacher. Beginning in adolescence, students must shift *five or more* times a day to several different teachers, each of whom has unique preferences about a myriad of aspects of their students' work.

The core ability students gain in doing that is the ability to rapidly perceive, interpret, and meet the expectations of authority figures. Is part of what is contributing to girls' success in school their ease with rule-following and adapting themselves to the preferences of those around them? Is that really something we want to celebrate?

This skill—of understanding and then adapting to what an authority figure wants—serves us in certain ways in our careers. We can glean what the boss wants and provide it. We can sense what would please an important mentor and act accordingly. Yet if we want to make a distinctive impact on our communities or organizations and make positive change, we need a different set of skills. We need to effectively *challenge authority,* not just adapt to it. We need to *influence* authority figures, not just please them.

Can you think of a time when you were asked to change your teacher's view on a subject and then rewarded for doing so effectively? Was *that* ever the assignment? Probably not: Challenging and influencing authority are not skills we're taught in traditional education, but they are critical skills for playing big.

A second problem with the school environment is that *a single authority figure* evaluates any given piece of student work—the class teacher. If I were to redesign school so that it helped both men and women play bigger, kids would sometimes turn in papers that would be graded, independently, by a few different teachers. They'd get back two or three or four assessments of their work, not just one. They could see what was common among those assessments and where teachers' opinions diverged. That much better reflects the landscape of our adult lives, where especially as they step into playing bigger, women are likely to find that some authority figures and influencers will appreciate what they are up to and some won't. Some will see their gifts and some won't. This method also teaches kids what we need to know as adults—that feedback often tells you about the preferences and priorities of the person giving it rather than giving you an objective assessment of the work itself.

Because of the single-authority-figure model we've gotten used to during our years in school, women often enter the work world believing the opinion of a current boss or mentor is absolute or objective. We fail to see the extent to which there will be a huge range of opinions on our work and a huge range of potential allies and mentors. Most important, we aren't used to discerning which authority figures we want to align ourselves with—a crucial skill. To play big, we need to evaluate which authority figures to seek out and cultivate as allies and which to move away from or simply ignore.

2. Preparation versus Improvisation

Doing well in a traditional academic environment is all about preparing. Think about the basic school paradigm: Study *in preparation* for the test, do the reading *in preparation* for the next day's discussion in class. Go home and work hard on that paper or project so that you'll get a good grade on it when you turn it in.

Imagine if a teacher gave a test on a topic he or she had never spoken a word about, a topic that wasn't on the syllabus or in the textbook. That would be considered unfair, because the implied paradigm at school is that *students will always have the opportunity to prepare in advance.*

Nothing could be further from the reality of our careers, where we are constantly called on to improvise, particularly as we move into more and more senior levels. We are asked difficult, unexpected questions we don't have the answers to, and we have to find a way to respond on our feet. Challenging situations we didn't anticipate and couldn't have prepared for arise, and we have to trust our ability to meet them.

This deep conditioning in the skill of preparation impacts women in particular. Studies have found that girls spend more time preparing their schoolwork than do boys. Even from a young age, preparation—and perhaps overpreparation—is a stronger behavior pattern in girls than in boys. Studies also show that when asked to prepare for a test or task as adults, women will spend more time preparing than men. One potential reason for this is bias. A host of studies show that because of subtle bias, women have to perform better than their male counterparts to be seen as performing equally. In response to this, women often work harder than their male counterparts, spending more time on preparatory work. In other words, we learn (consciously or unconsciously) that diligent preparation is a pretty good strategy for succeeding, as best we can, in a professional and academic world where we'll often be underestimated. The problem is, for many women, serious preparation isn't a strategy *they choose* when the situation requires it. It becomes a kind of default mode or habit they use all the time—causing them to waste a lot of time overpreparing and to avoid challenges that require improvisation, not preparation.

Women may also default to overpreparing and hard work because we are *less* likely to rely on other strategies for success. Studies show that many of the conventional strategies for workplace success don't work as well for women as they do for men—such as networking and explicitly advocating for oneself. Plus, some women feel uncomfortable using more traditional advancement strategies—like playing political games and using explicit self-promotion—because they don't feel they deserve to advance, or because advancing through those means strikes them as sleazy or nonmeritocratic. Whereas other advancement strategies seem unsavory, good preparation seems pure and fair.

Jane had always been a high-achieving student. After graduating from a prestigious university with an engineering degree, she went on to a management consulting job and then worked as an operations executive in a number of businesses. "I would come in, help put together the strategy, and build out the team that could execute it," she described. Midcareer, she pursued her long-held passion to bring her business expertise to the social sector and became the director of a small but full-of-potential nonprofit organization.

Jane was a serious preparer. She casually mentioned to me, as if it were nothing, that she spent four years studying up on the nonprofit sector, reading every book she could on fund-raising, board development, and nonprofit management so that she'd be prepared to seek a role in this new field. On the one hand, there's something beautiful and valuable about the humility with which Jane prepared to enter this new field. On the other hand, did Jane put her dreams on hold for longer than she needed to because her assumption was that the way to accomplish her goal was to be the ultimate good student, doing years of homework and studying so she'd know the answers to any question that might be asked on the test?

After a few months working at the nonprofit, Jane found she

was not enjoying her dream job in the way she had hoped because she was approaching it with perfectionism and an overpreparing habit. As a result, it was more stressful and less meaningful than she wanted it to be. It was at this time that she took the Playing Big course. Jane had already made the career change she aspired to but knew she needed to do some inner work to make the most of it.

She began taking courageous risks to move away from her old style of working. "At our recent board meeting, I approached things in a new way," she explained. "We are considering adding some new programs to what our organization offers. The old me would have brought this topic to the board only when I knew exactly what I thought we should do, the staffing needed, and a proposed rollout time line—in other words, when I'd prepared for months in good-student mode, researching, studying the issue, knowing my facts cold. Instead, this time I talked to the board about the general direction and how I thought we should go about the process of assessing the decision. It was so valuable, because the board honed in on the key questions we need to evaluate, and that will allow us to get to the right plan for us so much faster. It was out of my comfort zone to do it this way, but the group agreed that meeting was really one of our best." Jane is shifting out of the old way—good-student mode—to a broader set of leadership capacities that is more appropriate for her senior role. Now she is driving excellent performance in her organization by the processes she facilitates for her team and by acknowledging uncertainty and asking the right questions in the face of it.

3. Inside Out versus Outside In

If there's one thing I'd most like to change about school to help women play bigger, it's this: The dominant activity in school is absorbing information *from the outside*—whether from a book, a teacher's lecture, or the Internet—and then internalizing it. An overarching message is reinforced again and again through each sequence of (1) gather information from reading/lecture/research, (2) internalize information, (3) apply it on a paper, test, or presentation. That message is that the value we have to contribute on a topic *comes from information absorbed from an external source*—from the teacher's lecture, from the homework reading, from research.

Understandably, years of that conditioning leaves many adult women looking for the next degree or book or few hours of research to give them the answers they need for whatever task is before them. Yet playing big often requires the opposite: *accessing what we already know, trusting its value, and bringing it forth.* This is particularly true as women advance to senior levels in their careers, where they need to be the *source* of ideas and of thought leadership.

This is a complex issue for women, because in almost every professional field, the body of knowledge we absorb was shaped largely by male voices. In other words: *becoming competent = becoming educated = learning and internalizing what men have said about the subject for the past few hundred years.*

Being trained in a professional field, whether that field is law or engineering or medicine or business, entails learning a body of knowledge largely created by men, a body of knowledge based on men's experience and masculine norms. Succeeding in a field requires acting from that body of knowledge—alien or incomplete as it may seem. How does this affect women? And how can we expect women to enrich their fields with women's questions, perspectives, and ways of working if decades of school conditioning have taught them that the answer always lies outside, not within themselves?

What would school look like if it taught students both sets of skills equally: how to learn information from outside sources *and* how to draw on one's own creative ideas, insights, experience, and what one already knows? What if the typical school asked students not only to learn the existing body of knowledge on a subject but also to identify unasked questions, untested assumptions, voices and views neglected in that body of knowledge? That's what is required to teach students to innovate and to lead.

A second problem with the "outside-in" model of school is that it puts the emphasis on information: What matters in school, typically, is the *information* you've absorbed and how you apply it. While "what we know" remains important in our careers, it is only part of what is important. Equally if not more important are personal strengths like charisma, leadership, emotional intelligence, and problem-solving abilities that allow us to make a major impact in our careers. As Kalinda, a human resources consultant put it, "Often, before major client meetings, I get worried that I don't know enough about the topic we're discussing or that I'm giving a presentation about. I'll feel that sense of *pachad* and panic, telling myself I need to cram, reading up on the topic. But whenever I get feedback from my clients about why they work with me and my firm over the long term, they emphasize things like my candor, my strategic thinking, and my reliability. The truth is, when something comes up in a meeting that I don't know the information about, I can always go figure it out and report back." Good-student conditioning can cause us to assume our primary asset is what we know and to underestimate the potential impact of our innate strengths. It's time to retrain our brains: The value we bring doesn't just come from the information we've mastered. It also comes from *who we are*.

4. Just Do Good Work versus Do Good Work and Make It Visible

I was raised, as so many girls were, with the message "Get good grades in school, work hard, and you'll do well in your career." This narrative about the new meritocracy for women in the work world was a core message my generation and those who followed received—from our moms and from the media. The problem? It ignored a number of other factors that are critical for career success, one of them being self-promotion—making your work visible.

The idea that good work is enough is strongly reinforced in school, *because doing well in school does not require self-promotion*. It requires only doing quality work and handing it in to the teacher. Girls in school don't have to navigate the difficult territory that adult women do: being high achievers without threatening peers or coming across as unlikable, unfeminine. In school, girls can be excellent students via homework and test performance without their peers even knowing about that excellence. Yes, in some classes they also need to raise their hand and contribute in class, but they certainly don't need to speak about their academic accomplishments explicitly or advocate for themselves. This helps school fit squarely into girls' comfort zones—you can get the gold stars and be self-deprecating at the same time—but it leaves us totally unpracticed in the art of making our accomplishments visible when we land in the workplace. Compared to succeeding in the work world, it's relatively easy for girls to excel in school because they can do great work without having to defy feminine norms and navigate the likability costs that come with women's self-promotion.

Many women keep doing in their careers what they did in school: great, diligent work. We assume we're in a meritocratic environment and someone will reward us. Carol Frohlinger, an expert on women and negotiation, writes, "Symptoms include keeping your head down, delivering excellent work, expecting that people will notice—and eventually place a tiara on your head."

Research shows that men try to prove themselves in a job interview and initial negotiation—asking for higher pay and a more senior title at that stage—while women ask for less and plan to prove themselves on the job instead. Women often slowly realize their good work isn't leading to promotions or raises because it isn't sufficiently visible, on an ongoing basis, to those scouting talent within the organization or making decisions about career advancement. We start to understand, "Oh, in this workplace, I have to do good work *and* make it visible to the right people," but school hasn't taught us how to do that. In fact, it's made it all too easy for us to excel while avoiding ever speaking about our own accomplishments or abilities.

A Few Thoughts on Self-Promotion

Self-promotion is tricky for women, for a couple of reasons. Research shows that women incur social costs for advocating for themselves too strongly; they are seen as less likable by those around them, especially by other women. Yet studies also show that women who don't advocate for themselves at all are not seen as competent leaders. There is a tricky middle ground to find.

Second, many women feel turned off by the idea of self-promotion. I often hear women saying things along the lines of "Self-promotion is part of the same old bullshit organizational politics stuff I don't want to engage in. I don't want to play that game." I don't know too many women who hear the term "self-promotion" and say to themselves, "Yeah! I want to do more of that! That sounds just like my style! And that sounds just like what the world needs—more people doing more self-promotion!" For many women, the term connotes a kind of pumping up of one's ego; forced, awkward actions; and an effortful striving to be noticed.

A third issue that comes up for many women is the feeling that self-promoting is "masculine" and that career advice telling women to be more self-promoting is really just telling them to be "more like men." To that I say, think of a spunky, rambunctious five-year-old girl who has done something she's incredibly excited about. Maybe she wrote a song she's in love with. Maybe she mastered counting up to thirty, or maybe the garden she's been watering with her dad started to bloom and she's feeling quite proud. What would she do? She'd talk about that accomplishment, with pride. She'd want to show people. She hasn't yet learned to tamp down the way she talks about her accomplishments or learned that something about this instinct to share is dark, selfish, or wrong.

Of course, you aren't going to share about your accomplishments in the same way as a five-year-old, but thinking about her helps us remember that wanting to share our creations, ideas, and successes is not the domain of the masculine—it's the domain of the free. There's a delight and fun in it, and it's what we *all* do before some of us are taught to do otherwise.

Here are three ways to think about self-promotion that may feel less sleazy, less uncomfortable, less detrimental to others, and more aligned with your values:

1. Drop the idea of "self-promotion" and think about the concept of *visibility* instead. How can your talents and accomplishments and ideas become more visible to audiences, influencers, and decision makers within your organization or your field? When you shift the frame to visibility, you'll notice it's not all about you. Instead, it becomes about making *your work and ideas* available to those who can utilize them.

2. Focus on service. Ask yourself, How can I make my work more visible to audiences, influencers, and decision makers so that I can reach those I want to serve? Your TEDx talk or op-ed article about your hard-earned lessons or ideas can help others. Posting on your company's intranet or hosting a brown-bag lunch at your office about the innovative process your team has been using makes your accomplishments more visible *and* allows other teams to benefit. Sharing your ideas about potential improvements for the processes at the hospital where you work showcases your good thinking *and* can make a positive impact for the patients you serve.

3. Think about telling the whole truth. Women tell many little lies—lies of omission—about their accomplishments. For many women, it's helpful to think about "telling the whole truth" rather than about self-promoting. Do you "lie" in any of these ways?

- Always giving credit to others on a team while not acknowledging your own role
- Communicating about areas of a project where you fell short, but not communicating equally about areas of success
- Never mentioning extra work or off hours spent on a project

- Not highlighting past accomplishments, education, awards—even when they are highly relevant
- Rationalizing away past accomplishments, education, or awards ("that award was kind of silly anyway," "that degree isn't so relevant here," "I only got that special assignment in my last job because they needed someone to fill a gap immediately")
- Confusing the personal path of turning away from external status markers with the devaluing of what one has accomplished (for example, leaving corporate law and transitioning to a social sector job and no longer acknowledging the remarkable accomplishment of making partner at a prestigious law firm, or taking one's art in a less commercial direction and talking in a diminishing way about that art having been featured on the cover of a major magazine)

It's good to get comfortable with self-promotion because, yes, it's important for professional success. But I'm more interested in something deeper: how speaking forthrightly about our accomplishments allows women to *know our accomplishments and integrate them into our sense of self*. In other words, if we never hear ourselves owning—or even hinting at—what we've overcome, created, nurtured, or completed in our lives, how can we know competence, strength, and resilience as part of who we are? How does what we are and aren't willing to say about ourselves affect our sense of self?

Good-Student Skills	Playing Big Skills
Adapting to authority figures	Adapting to authority when necessary/strategic but also . . . • challenging authority • influencing authority • identifying which authority figures to cultivate alliances with and which to ignore
Preparation	Preparation and improvisation
Turning outward for knowledge	Turning outward for knowledge at times, but often turning inward and trusting what you already know
Heads-down good work	Doing good work and making that work visible

Changes to Help You Play Bigger

As you've been reading, you've probably begun to recognize some of the good-student habits that hinder you and some of the new, complementary abilities you need to develop to support your playing bigger. You can continue to use your good-student skill set as a foundation for doing quality work while also learning to paint with new colors. The four days of practices and journaling questions that follow are a great way to begin making those changes for yourself.

From School to Work				
	The Old Skill What was rewarded in school	**The New Skill** What you need to play bigger	**Today's Challenge**	**My Report**
Relating to authority	As a student, you got really good at figuring out what each authority figure wanted and providing it.	Now, in your career, you need to . . . • challenge and influence authority figures; • find alternative authority figures aligned with your point of view; • become the authority figure.	Find one opportunity to influence an authority figure in your industry or organization.	**What I Did:** **What I Learned:** **What I Want to Do with This Next:**
Preparation versus improvisation	In school, you learned how to prepare: how to be ready with the answer for anything you might be asked.	Brilliant careers require that we think on our feet. At work, prepare, but be careful not to overprepare out of fear or insecurity, and get used to the idea that improvising is part of your job description.	Look for a situation that calls for you to act on your feet. Instead of avoiding it or retreating into preparation, improvise.	**What I Did:** **What I Learned:** **What I Want to Do with This Next:**

	The Old Skill	The New Skill	Today's Challenge	My Report
	What was rewarded in school	What you need to play bigger		
Inside out versus outside in	School taught you how to look outside yourself for the answers.	As you move to more and more senior levels in your career, you'll need to turn your focus inward and trust what you already know.	Find one opportunity today where your instinct is to look outside yourself for the answers and, instead, take a few deep breaths, slow down, and look inside to see what ideas and insights are already in you. Bring those forward.	**What I Did:** **What I Learned:** **What I Want to Do with This Next:**
Just do good work versus do good work and make it visible	In school you learned that if you worked hard and performed well, you'd get a good grade.	Work hard, but make sure people know about your excellent performance. Find your way to own your accomplishments and talk about them gracefully.	Today, gracefully share one of your professional accomplishments with people at work in a way that feels comfortable for you.	**What I Did:** **What I Learned:** **What I Want to Do with This Next:**

Journaling Questions

. . . .

What new relationship to authority is required for your playing bigger?

What kinds of improvising do you need to do as you start playing bigger? What kinds of situations are likely to arise that will require you to act on your feet, without time to prepare?

If you know you've got an overpreparing habit, how might your career look different if you spent 20 percent less time preparing diligently and used that time for taking bold risks and playing bigger stretches in your career?

Where are you turning outward, thinking that more information is what you need, when really you've got lots of answers and ideas already inside?

How are your personal strengths and lived experiences—not just the information you've learned—part of what allows you to make a meaningful contribution?

How can you make your work and ideas more visible in ways that would also serve others in your organization or field or who are part of an audience you'd like to impact?

The Big Ideas

1. Girls' success in school is widely celebrated, but we need to look critically at this success and recognize the overlap between "good-girl" norms and the behaviors rewarded in school.

2. Traditional schooling gives women many important skills, but it doesn't teach many of those most essential for leadership.

3. As women transition from student mode to career, they must add to their tool kit:

   - The ability to challenge authority
   - The ability to improvise
   - The ability to draw on and trust what they already know
   - The ability to make their work visible to others

CHAPTER 6

• • •

Hiding

I n this chapter, I'm going to call you out. *Lovingly* call you out, that is. We're going to talk about the ways brilliant women hide from playing bigger—the ways we stall on and talk ourselves out of the very steps that would bring us more fulfillment and enable us to have more positive impact in the world. All these "hiding strategies" allow us to avoid playing bigger *while* convincing ourselves we're moving forward in the most diligent way we can. After all, these are *brilliant* women's hiding strategies: We are sophisticated in fooling ourselves.

A warning: Typically when I introduce women to these hiding moves, they have some "uh-oh" moments as they see the unconscious ways they've been procrastinating on playing bigger. So be forewarned, and be kind to yourself.

Hiding Strategy #1: This before That

"This before that" are the false beliefs we hold about *the order* in which things need to happen: "I'd love to teach classes on *x* topic, but first I have to save up the money for a web designer, because I need a website about my classes before I can teach." Or "I'd love to invite so-and-so awesome senior executive at my company to lunch, but I can't do it yet, because first I need to get more clarity on what I want my next career step to be, so I know how to steer the conversation."

We come up with *tons* of these stories about sequencing around our playing big. The problem is, they are usually false. You don't need to have a website to teach a course. You don't need to know your career direction before you have lunch with that senior woman you admire. In fact, the lunch with her might help you figure it out.

One of my favorite examples of how "this before that" can get us stuck is from Hannah, a technology consultant and mom of three. Hannah has a gregarious personality and a love for travel. For Hannah, playing big meant seeing more of the world, exposing her children to new places, and doing her work in a different culture than the northeastern United States. She was interested in moving to Japan with her family and working there for a few years.

"Okay, so what's your next step?" I asked Hannah. She answered that she was working as hard as she could and as fast as she could to get to that dream by . . . drum roll, please . . . taking Japanese language classes twice a week.

I was a little perplexed. Hannah explained, "Well, to work there I need to know the language, so I've been taking Japanese for two years, but it's hard to squeeze in the time to study between my job and the kids. I think I need at least two more years of classes before my language would be good enough."

"Do you have any evidence you need to master the language to get a job in your field in Japan?" I asked her. "Tomorrow, what if you were to contact three companies you might want to work for there and see what opportunities exist for English speakers with your skill set? Maybe living in Japan really isn't contingent on spending years learning the language."

Hannah could suddenly see how she'd invented a limiting story about sequencing that let her stay in her comfort zone. As much as she wanted to go to Japan, she was also afraid of the big change, afraid people wouldn't get why she was going, afraid because taking action around this dream evoked both *pachad* and *yirah*.

After our conversation, she began networking and reaching out to potential employers to see if there might be a way to make the move right away. It turned out there were several opportunities, and she made plans to relocate in time for her kids to start at Japanese schools in the following academic year.

You might be wondering, How could Hannah not see for herself that she might not need to know the language? Don't be so quick to judge. The "this before that" beliefs we hold often seem obviously false—even ridiculous—to outsiders but very plausible to us. When it comes to your playing bigger, are you holding an assumption that in order to do x, first you need to do y? Do you have any evidence to back up that assumption? Is it possible you can take a more direct route?

Hiding Strategy #2: Designing at the Whiteboard

Picture a small team of bright people coming up with good ideas in their company conference room, writing notes and bullet points on a whiteboard. Then, the team goes forward and develops plans based on those ideas. What's wrong with that? Sounds like good work, right?

In Silicon Valley parlance, when a company develops a product or service in this way—*without outside feedback from customers or other relevant stakeholders*—it's called "designing at the whiteboard." Designing at the whiteboard *seems* like a reasonable way to get work done, but it generally brings disaster. It's too easy for the insiders, the people passionate about and committed to a product, to veer into fantasyland as they make their plans.

Designing at the whiteboard could be planning a retreat for your team at work without consulting your colleagues on the agenda. Designing at the whiteboard could be sitting alone at your computer for hours revamping your résumé for a job search without any real information about what hiring managers for your desired position are looking for. Designing at the whiteboard could be spending week after week thinking about branding for the small business you want to start without ever talking to your ideal customer to see if it resonates with them. In other words, designing at the whiteboard is any brainstorming, business-building, or creative process that you pursue in isolation—without feedback from the people you are trying to reach with your creation.

When we design at the whiteboard, we *feel* as if we are doing diligent work, but much of that work turns out to be unproductive, because what we create isn't aligned with what our intended audience wants. Our creations flop because they are too untethered from the reality of the people we are trying to reach.

Let me tell you about Lena, a gifted young writer and, by day, a research assistant in a cognitive science laboratory. Lena had been working on an incredible project: a children's book about the human brain. She was passionate about making complex neurological concepts accessible to kids in storybook form so that they could grow up with a greater understanding of how their minds work.

Lena was feeling stuck. She'd worked on this book, carefully, enthusiastically for years, and now the content was done, but she wasn't sure how to take it forward. It could go a couple of different directions—illustrated book, text only, digital—and, she told me, "I don't know which format is best, and everything else I need to do depends on that." She sounded stressed.

The first thing I said to Lena was no wonder she was stressed! She was personally trying to answer a question about the format that *she* couldn't answer. There was no way Lena could know which format was right because only her *intended audience* could tell her which format worked best for them. We had to get Lena out of designing-at-the-whiteboard mode, which she'd been in for years, and into contact with her desired readership for the book.

With a little coaching, Lena identified her ideal readers as eight-to ten-year-old girls with an interest in science. We made a plan for her to share the draft material with about ten girls in that age group and get their feedback: Did they like it? What did they take away from the book? What page did they get up to? How quickly did they read it? Did any of them try to share it with friends? All this would help Lena understand how to improve what she'd created. We also came up with a plan in which she'd give some girls a version of the book with more artwork, others a version with less, some a hard copy, and some digital—in effect market testing what format worked best.

This might sound like an anecdote about the importance of doing market research, but it's more than that. It's about the penchant so many brilliant women have to work conscientiously on their creations in relative isolation, not testing them or exposing them to feedback along the way.

The whiteboard is safe for us. It's cozy because it doesn't expose our ideas to criticism or rejection. We don't discover any facts that conflict with our plans. But the whiteboard can also be lonely and disorienting. We can get lost creating and revising there. It's also subtly anxiety provoking, because when we design at the whiteboard, like Lena, we ask ourselves to do an impossible task: to make every creative decision correctly instead of experimenting and learning what works for the audience we want to reach.

When I asked Lena, "How does it feel to contemplate showing your book to those ten young girls—this week?" she replied, "Really scary, and really great. Kind of exhilarating." This is how it feels to step away from the whiteboard and test our creations and ideas with those we want to reach: It evokes both fear and excitement—the *yirah* of playing bigger now. Within a few weeks, Lena had gathered valuable feedback on her book, knew which steps to take next, and, perhaps most important, was feeling a renewed sense of commitment to taking the project forward.

Hiding Strategy #3: Overcomplicating and Endless Polishing

Gina had always believed that adversity could be transformed and used for good. So after going through breast cancer, she asked herself, What can I do out of this experience that will serve others? A business process consultant from Ann Arbor (with a love for antiquing on the side), Gina had found that a set of daily rituals—writing a gratitude list, having a regular check-in call with friends, yoga, and a morning intention-setting practice—helped her get through each day of cancer treatment. She wanted to share with other breast cancer patients about the activities and routines that had helped her cope.

At first, Gina envisioned a short, web-based guide, but then she thought, "Gosh, it would be really wonderful to have the rituals integrated in a special day planner women could buy. In fact, yes, some kind of physical product will really help this get traction. The day planner is essential. Also, there should be a place on the website where women could discuss the ideas with each other! And we need some way for them to add in their own daily ritual ideas—some kind of collaborative, interactive discussion space." Suddenly Gina was overwhelmed by the work, technical complexity, and expense involved. She stopped moving forward.

Gina was unconsciously using the hiding strategy of overcomplicating—adding element after element to her creation so that she never had to finish and put her work out into the world. Usually when we're using this strategy, we're convinced all the complications and additions are *essential*. Of course, sometimes additional elements are truly needed, but often our fears about playing bigger find cover under the conviction that we have to build something large and complex.

If you know that you sometimes fall into this habit, start noticing how effective *simple* can be. You'll find examples everywhere. Think about products you love that are quite simple. Think about thriving businesses that offer one basic product or service. Think about writers you admire who've authored successful and impactful books that, at their core, have one simple thesis. Simple can be more than enough, but because so many brilliant women are used to overperforming in order to be seen as equally capable as their male counterparts, that can be hard for us to believe.

Endless *polishing*, a cousin to overcomplicating, is getting stuck in so-called improving each element of a creation before putting it out into the world: endless revising of the essay, more research to back up the speech, more revision of the design, and so on.

I know: You want your work to be high quality. Brilliant women do. But we have to be rigorous about distinguishing when our "commitment to quality" is just a fancy cover for our fears. Our good-student conditioning tells us that the more perfected something is (in our own eyes), the better. Plus, like most women, you may have gotten used to trying to perfect your work before anyone sees it. That may have been effective in other circumstances, but when it comes to playing bigger, sometimes getting it done is more important than polishing.

How do you know when your revisions or additions are really important and when they are not worth the time—or are even making your creation worse—in the eyes of your customer or audience? That's where feedback comes in—you need to hear from your target audience that the polishing or additions are necessary in their eyes, rather than letting your inner critic decide they are imperative. Is it possible that the simple version, the existing version, is already good enough—at least good enough to take beyond the whiteboard?

Hiding Strategy #4: Collecting and Curating Everyone *Else*'s Ideas

A few years ago, a woman in Playing Big wrote this in our online discussion forum:

> "I have worked as a researcher and policy advisor in Afghanistan for the last decade or so. I'm considered an expert

in my field, and have been successful in it. Yet I often feel a sense of futility about my work—how limited my power in this role really is, and how exhausting and hopeless it can feel to work to change something I perhaps can't really change."

When I read this, I thought, What a fascinating topic and important theme: the sense of futility that those working on our society's most intractable and heartbreaking problems often feel, and what to do about it. I also thought about how well positioned this woman was to write and speak about it, as an expert in the field of international development who had felt that sense of futility herself.

Then, I read what came next:

"As my next step, I plan to interview colleagues in my field about this topic, to see if others share this feeling, and perhaps put together some kind of project based on their perspectives."

I've seen so many women make this move. A woman becomes captivated by an idea. She's captivated because she's noticed something missing from the conversation and has something to say. Yet instead of sharing her own perspective, she creates a project to curate *other* people's ideas about it.

Of course, sometimes projects like these are needed. Sometimes, a woman's true calling includes "gathering the voices" on a topic. Other times, collecting others' perspectives serves as a needed stepping-stone that helps her discover her own. But far more often, brilliant women feature others' ideas to sidestep claiming their own thought leadership. Turning outward to "gather the voices" is often a fear-based but good-looking escape from taking the simple, scary step of sharing one's own voice now.

Hiding Strategy #5: Omitting Your Own Story

Jacqueline was a professor of public health at a prestigious university. Her research and teaching focused on child abuse treatment and intervention. Jacqueline had suffered a violent childhood herself, but she had never uttered a word to her colleagues or her students about that. As Jacqueline developed a relationship with her inner mentor, she could see how including her story in her professional life was important—for her own integrity, and to stay focused on the aim that was at the heart of her work: reducing the number of children growing up in terror.

Jacqueline started a practice of telling some of her personal story in one of the early days of class each semester. In her academic talks, she did something quite unheard-of: She began mentioning an episode from her own life that illustrated a research finding she was speaking about. She became known not just as a scholar, but also as an advocate for the issue and a model of overcoming adversity. She started getting opportunities that made her work more influential on a broader scale, and she started to find more meaning in her interactions with colleagues and students.

The firm division of the professional and the personal, the "objective expert" persona, the delusion that the work we are drawn to has nothing to do with the core questions in our hearts—these are outdated ideas. A new way is possible, a way that acknowledges that when we have the privilege to choose our work, we move toward topics that matter deep within our souls. In this model, there are no perfectly objective experts who are the ultimate authorities on their subjects but rather a diversity of people who have worked deeply in an area and who each bring to their topics a very subjective, partial view—a subjectivity inevitably colored by their personalities and life experiences. When we truly acknowledge that, we can take off some of the professional masks we wear. We let go of personas that don't serve any of us. We can say, Here's my experience; here's why my work really matters to me; and here are my ideas, questions, research findings, offerings on this topic. Here's what I can bring to the mosaic; what about you? Even when our work is informed by research and professional expertise, like Jacqueline's is, it gains power and resonance when we remove the mask and imbue it with a vulnerable sharing about *why* it matters to us.

Playing bigger always includes, in some way, coming forward to tell our own tales; voice our own questions; and share our bare, simple truths. This is how our work finds its spark and gains the power not just to inform minds but also to change hearts.

In my own life, I used hiding strategy #4 (collecting and curating everyone else's ideas) and strategy #5 (omitting my own story) in combination. A few times during my childhood, my parents joined synagogues and enrolled me in Hebrew school. Each time I'd watch the men in front of the congregation reading and giving speeches and I'd wonder, Why can't women go up there too? The people they were reading and giving speeches about were men too, it seemed. I remember feeling as if I was supposed to be invisible, as if I was unwanted there, in this place that was about God and history and everything important.

A decade later, I went off to college and encountered a very different Jewish community. I took classes with a woman rabbi and read about the women of the Bible. I learned about the changes happening in many aspects of Jewish life—from the marriage ceremony to the Shabbat prayers—that were making Judaism more inclusive for women. After college, when I was in my early twenties, I worked with that rabbi and another recent graduate to create an anthology of Jewish women's writings. The collection added women's perspectives into a liturgy long dominated by male voices and featured over two hundred contributing authors—from Supreme Court Justice Ruth Bader Ginsburg to activist Eve Ensler.

I recruited authors. I helped match them with subjects for their essays. I edited and edited and edited their work. Yet when it came time to write my own essay for the book, I procrastinated. I hesitated to put my own ideas out there. When I finally did write it, just a couple of weeks before the manuscript was due, I skipped the heart of the matter: my story, why I was doing this project, what it was like to be that little girl growing up in synagogue, feeling that sense of being unwanted. I took refuge in a cerebral essay that seemed appropriate from the vantage point of my "good-student" conditioning, but that I now know was much less powerful than what I could have written.

That story of what it was like to be the young girl in synagogue was my slice of the truth to tell. That was a story the Jewish community needed to hear. That was the experience life had chosen to give me, the story it had brought through me, and the real reason I was working on the anthology. Sure, there were some playing bigger stretches for me in creating and publishing the collections of other people's work, but the deeper playing big would have come from also sharing my story in the book.

"My slice of the truth to tell" is an important phrase in our journeys to playing bigger. Can we resist the fear-based tendency to make our work abstract or overly complex and instead trust that our lived experiences, insights, and natural ideas are enough to bring to the table? Often, *that* kind of authenticity and vulnerability is what is needed to move hearts and create change. Quite often, that is also what will cause us to be noticed, to be respected, and to receive the opportunities we desire.

There is an unexpected connection between staying right-size and playing big. Playing big often comes from standing within our story, mundane as it may seem to us. Ironically, playing *small* often shows up in projects that look big and ambitious—as it did for me with the anthology—because in all the bigness, there's lots of room to hide from personal visibility, from saying what one really has to say.

Hiding Strategy #6: I Need the Degree . . .

One of the most common hiding strategies is also one of the easiest to overlook, because it's something we generally regard as a good idea: getting more (and more and more) education. Naturally, there are good reasons to pursue postgraduate education. School is a great way to develop one's critical-thinking skills. It can be a good place to network and meet others with similar interests. Advanced degrees increase earning power and competitiveness in the job market, and, certainly, going to school can be personally enriching. Sometimes school teaches very specific information and skills we need to do a job: If you aspire to be a surgeon or civil rights attorney or a hospice nurse, you need a specific education. *All these* are sound reasons to pursue more education: to boost one's salary, to network, to develop critical-thinking skills, to get technical training for a specific kind of work, or simply for the intellectual stimulation and community.

Yet often, brilliant women seek out more education for another reason: because getting the next training or degree is within our psychological comfort zone, and leaping into playing bigger right now is not. Talented women with a dream believe that they *need* another degree, training, or certification because they are not "enough" as they are. They look to an external qualification to give them a sense of internal permission to lead and create. They assume that more education will transform their fears into easy confidence—even though, in truth, education has never done that for them before. It just puts confronting those fears on hold for a few years. School makes it easy to convince ourselves we are moving forward, doing something very productive (after all, what's more legitimized in our culture than getting more education?), when in fact we're delaying playing bigger.

Playing Big graduate Carol Anne Wall, a reporting analyst and adjunct writing professor, put it this way: "I thought I would apply to graduate school and get a second master's, but I realized that I was using education as a reason to stall the process of what I really want to do—write, build websites, and teach. More graduate school wouldn't help me with that and would probably take away from those things. I need to leap from where I am, not wait for a better-educated me."

Another client, Annie, loved her job as a literacy specialist for young kids. She had a second vocation, one that came alive during the summers, working as a counselor at a camp that she'd attended as a child. For years, Annie daydreamed about creating an outdoor education program to teach kids reading. She could picture the whole thing in her mind's eye: the activities the group would do, how it would work, and where she could hold the program.

"Sounds fabulous," I said to Annie. "What's the next step?"

"Well, I don't think I can really do this," she said, "because I don't have a degree in outdoor education. I'm really not trained for this."

I asked Annie what training she did have. Well, she did have that master's degree in early childhood education, she explained. Plus certification as a reading specialist . . . and then there was her decades of experience as a camp counselor.

By the time Annie had walked me through all that, she got the point: She really did have adequate training to do this. As we probed a bit deeper, it became clear to both of us that her fears about creating this new program were finding cover in the excuse "But I need that other degree."

Leadership and team development expert Stacey Sargeant has observed this hiding strategy so much in herself that she's even come up with a slogan for it: "I'd better get a PhD in that." She explains:

"My colleague Jan Gelman and I often partner in leading workshops. One time, some participants in our workshop talked about the challenges of working in a male-dominated industry—gaming. Jan and I were both trained in an awareness practice called Process Work, and we talked about bringing Process Work focused on 'Rank and Power' into the workshop, thinking it would be very useful to the group.

"We'd both taken several trainings in Process Work, studying with the president of the Process Work Institute. Yet as we thought about the idea, we hesitated: *Did we really know enough to do the exercises well? Perhaps we should get the president to come in instead? Maybe we needed to take a few more workshops first?*

"Once we realized what we were saying to one another, we laughed at how it had happened again. We'd fallen into telling ourselves, 'I better get a PhD in it first,' before we even so much as used some theories in our teaching!

"'I better get a PhD in it first' has become our joke. Jan and I both have master's degrees in applied behavioral science focusing on organizational systems, as well as a long list of other education; we are well qualified for our work! Now that we're aware of our habit of questioning our expertise, we recognize it, throw out the (ironic) mantra 'I need another PhD,' laugh, and move forward. We shift into what we *do* know. We remember what we hear again and again from our clients: What serves them best is our own authenticity and experience, our sharing of ourselves."

If you've got the education-seeking habit, have compassion for yourself. In our formative childhood years, most of us got the message (from the basic model of school itself) that the value we bring to the world comes from what we've just learned from a book or a teacher rather than from what we already know or our life's experience. It's no wonder that when we want to bring something into the world, our reflex is to look outward for the next kind of education to prepare us to do so. The school environment is an appealing safe harbor for the parts of us that fear stepping into playing bigger. Excessive education allows us to put off the scary work of stepping into our roles as leaders, creators, and change agents while all the while convincing us it is actually preparing us to step into those roles.

Ways We Hide and Delay Playing Bigger	Ways We Become Visible and Start Playing Bigger Right Now
This then that	Recognizing there are many possible orders in which the steps to one's goal can happen, and choosing the most direct route to playing bigger right now
Designing at the whiteboard	Designing in conversation with the intended audience
Overcomplicating and endless polishing	A simple bold creation Sharing an early version to learn what needs to be improved on in the customers'/audience's/stakeholders' eyes
Collecting or curating what everyone else has to say about it	Sharing what you have to say about the topic
Omitting your own story	Including your own story and why the work matters to you
Getting more and more and more education	Sharing what you already know

Journaling Questions

....

Here are the hiding strategies we explored in this chapter:

- *Limiting stories about sequencing*
- *Designing at the whiteboard*
- *Overcomplicating*
- *Endless polishing*
- *Collecting/curating what others have to say instead of sharing your own perspective*
- *Skipping over your own story*
- *Getting more and more education, training, certifications (or doing endless research)*

What are the top three that have been holding you back?

1.
2.
3.

How are these showing up in your life or career right now?

Now that you are aware of them, how might you approach things differently?

The Big Ideas

1. Brilliant women commonly hide from and postpone their own playing bigger by:

    -   Having false assumptions about the order that things need to happen.
    -   Designing at the whiteboard, untethered from conversations with the audiences we want to reach.
    -   Collecting and highlighting *other people's* thoughts about a topic we are passionate about rather than sharing our own ideas.
    -   Creating something overly complex or abstract while omitting our own personal story.
    -   Seeking ever more education, training, or certifications—convincing ourselves we need the degree in order to play bigger.
    -   Doing endless feature polishing and elaboration.

2. Ironically, we often play small through projects that appear big and ambitious, because in all that bigness, there is lots of room to bury our own voices and ideas.

CHAPTER 7

• • •

Leaping

In the previous chapter, we explored the common ways brilliant women hide from playing bigger. In this chapter, you'll learn about the antidote to these forms of hiding—a special kind of action I call leaping. Leaps get us playing bigger *right now*.

Susan longed to leave her job in corporate finance and open a gourmet food business. Her leap was to host a one-day "gourmet food market" in her backyard. She selected products, crafted a marketing announcement, and invited people in her social circle as well as some relevant community groups. Her leap had big benefits—both emotional and strategic. It gave Susan an immediate, motivating taste of working in the area of her passion—she felt a huge increase in her energy level both as she prepared for it and afterward. She went into the leap with some questions about what kinds of products were available and what would sell well with her target customers. She learned a lot about those questions—and that helped her refine her plans for the business.

A leap action meets these six criteria:

1. It gets you playing bigger now, according to what playing bigger means to you.
2. It can be finished within one to two weeks.
3. It's simple: an action that you could describe in a short phrase. For example, "host a workshop," "send a memo to my boss about my strategy ideas," "apply to three jobs in my desired field."
4. It gets your adrenaline flowing, because a leap stretches you out of your comfort zone. No adrenaline, no little tinge of *yirah?* Then the action you're contemplating isn't a leap.
5. A leap puts you in contact with the audience you want to reach or influence. Leaps cannot be done in isolation. Coming up with the strategy for your team's new product launch is not a leap. Writing the mission statement for the nonprofit you want to start is not a leap. Identifying the list of people you want to invite to be on the board of your company is not a leap. These are all great actions—they may feel exciting and move your project forward, *but they are not leaps* because they do not involve contact between you and those you want to influence. Coming up with the strategy for your team's new product launch *and* sharing it with the key stakeholders for the launch is a leap. Writing the mission statement for your nonprofit *and* holding a meeting to get feedback on it from your potential major donors is a leap. Identifying who you want to invite

to be on the board of your company *and* calling up a prospective board member to invite him or her—*those* constitute leaps.

6. You leap with an intent to learn. There are many reasons for leaping—to get yourself to act, to experience the joy of playing bigger right away—but the most important reason to leap is to learn. Leaps work best when you approach them with a question you want answered by taking the leap. For example, if your leap is inviting that prospective member to join your board, the curious question might be, "Is my pitch to board members working?" If your leap is sharing your blog with some people in your target audience, the question might be, "Is this material engaging the readers I want to engage?"

Think, for a moment, about what playing bigger looks like for you right now. Now, what's an action you could take that meets the six criteria above? That's a leap.

Leap Stories

Leaps can be hard to understand at first, so let me tell you a leap story. Here's how Laura Grisolano, an attorney who wanted to start a mediation practice, described her leap:

"I've been held back from starting my own mediation practice by using so many of the 'hiding strategies' we've talked about. I've been waiting on more education and research,

needing all the pieces to be perfect before the reveal, doing excessively detailed planning, and what I called 'chicken/egg' problems: I can't do *a* without *b* and I can't do *b* without *a!*

"Hearing about these hiding strategies has helped me discover that I don't need to wait any longer. My leap is to stop looking for the perfect web designer and, in the next two weeks, build a very simple social media page for the mediation practice. It will force me to put all the pieces in one place, in a very simplified version. It will give me, in effect, a 'brochure' to which I can refer potential clients. In terms of learning, doing this will help me gather feedback that will inform my eventual website. I'm also going to focus on fleshing out just one service for now—not my entire line of offerings. My focus on building the perfect website was taking me further away from doing the work I want to do. This leap will move me closer."

And here's how Debbie Lamb Turner described her leap:

"My big dream is to have an amazing retreat center for hope, healing, and infinite possibilities. In addition to using it for my women's retreats, it would be available for other facilitators to use with their own programs that inspire and empower. My leap is to begin that process now, before I actually have the building. I scheduled a get-together at my home in April for women to meet, be supported, and be empowered. I am sending out the information about it in my newsletter tomorrow. So exciting—and scary—just putting it out there."

Debbie found a quick, inexpensive way to move forward. It didn't reflect her full, ideal vision—the retreat center—but it did enable her to get to the heart of what she really wanted to do right away, which was create healing spaces for women. It also allowed her to learn about what kind of woman was drawn to her gatherings, what elements were most successful, and what elements needed some tweaking.

Carrie wanted to write and publish a memoir. She'd been writing for many years, and what she really wanted—getting her story out there—felt very far away. Her leap was to write a short personal essay that recounted one important episode from her life and to send it to a magazine for publication. She gave herself ten days to write a story and a cover note, and then submit it to a magazine she thought would be a great fit. Carrie's leap gave her an immediate pathway to fulfill that core longing to get her voice out. It also pushed her to confront the fears that were causing her to stall on her book project, because those same fears came up, strongly, when she was crafting the essay for publication. Carrie had to take three such leaps—submitting her work to three different publications—before she found the right fit, but this meant that within a few months she had secured publication for her essay and was living her dream, not waiting to do so. On a more practical level, she learned a lot about polishing and submitting her writing and about what kinds of publications were responsive to her work.

Why Leap?

As you can see from these stories, there are many reasons to leap. There are **tactical reasons:** Leaps make you more effective. You learn more quickly what does and does not resonate with your au-

The Old Way	The Leap Way
Write a book over the next year.	Write an article/blog post/manifesto this week, submit it next week, and learn about what resonates with my audience or about which publications are/aren't a good fit for my work.
Read one hundred books and compile research.	Speak from my personal experience and what I know so far. Learn about what my core message is around this topic and who it seems to resonate with.
Spend the next six months developing a workshop.	E-mail my friends and family today about a pilot workshop I'll hold in two weeks. Sit down and sketch it out in an hour. Learn from the RSVPs what kind of person is interested in this workshop.
Have a long design process for a fancy website.	Get a free website in the next fifteen minutes. Write two different "about" pages this week and send them to ten people in my target market, asking them to give feedback on which resonates with them more. Put up the winning "about" page on my site by next week. Learn, from this leap, what kind of bio/introduction resonates best with my audience.

dience. You confront practical obstacles sooner, so you can address them or change your plans accordingly before you've invested a great deal of time and effort. You get more practice at whatever it is you want to do (since a leap has you actually *doing* it) and improve your skills.

There are also **psychological reasons to leap.** When you contemplate a leap, you evoke your *pachad* fears: fear of failure, rejection, or feeling not good enough; fears of change, of success, of shining so bright you'll feel separate from the herd. These fears aren't caused by leaping; they are *revealed* through leaping. These are the same old fears that have kept you playing small all along. Now you've drawn them up above the surface and can work through them, using the tools you've learned for shifting out of *pachad*.

Above all, I think the greatest benefit of leaping is the joy. Leaps pull us into self-actualization, into living the life of our inner mentor, into pursuing our passions *now*. Instead of writing the business plan, you're making and selling your first product and learning the truth about what should be a part of your plan. Instead of dreaming of publishing a book, you get to share your story in a column for your local paper, right now. That unleashes joy, energy, a sense of meaning, and, of course, *yirah*. Leaping changes your concept of self from *I want to be a woman who . . .* to *This is who I am.* Artist and creativity coach Melissa Dinwiddie put it this way, after she and a colleague held their first workshop, leap-style: "Having done it once, our self-identity has shifted from '*we want* to run creativity workshops in inspiring locations' to 'we *do* run creativity workshops in inspiring locations!' This has been an object lesson in just doing it."

Why Not Leap?

Despite all these benefits, we resist leaping because it makes us feel vulnerable and evokes the uncomfortable sensations of *pachad* and *yirah*. Sharing early, messy versions of our creations and ideas can feel excruciating—especially for those of us who are used to perfecting and polishing our work. We also avoid leaps because they force us to confront uncomfortable realities about our visions: You might discover that you really don't want to pursue the dream you thought you were destined for. You might find your audience really doesn't want what you create. Leaps also push us to do the very unsexy sharing of our work in a mundane way with a small crowd—not with the grand audience and splashy start we may have imagined. For all these reasons, we resist leaps.

A Few Notes on Leaping

When it comes to leaping, here's what *doesn't* work well: taking the bold action of a leap and, if it doesn't work out how you wanted, feeling like a failure. But it's actually just as problematic to simply celebrate if the leap went well and then move on. No matter what the outcome is, leaps should be used for learning.

The leap of writing the draft chapter of your book and sharing it with your ideal reader might have this learning question at its heart: *Based on the feedback I get from these three readers, am I communicating what I intend to communicate through these words?* The learning questions at the heart of a brainstorming meeting with your target donors for your nonprofit might include: *What aspects of this mission statement resonate more and which resonate less with these donors? What will it take to gain their financial support?* Focusing on the learning goal of the leap helps us understand what to do with the results of the leap: Interpret the learning and use it to inform our next leap.

Get Feedback from the People You Want to Influence and Reach

A leap must expose your work to your intended audience. When you design a leap, first identify the people you want to reach or influence through your playing big and gather their feedback specifically. As discussed in the chapter on praise and criticism, in almost every case, the important feedback won't come from your friends, family members, supportive cheerleaders in your life, or even from mentors and advisors. It will come from customers in the case of a business, your desired readers, viewers or listeners in the case of art, investors or donors if your task has to do with raising money. You can go to friends and family for support, but they are not going to be able to tell you what works or what doesn't about your plan because they are not representative of your desired audience.

Interpret Feedback

People usually don't know exactly what they want—which is why survey data or focus groups are notoriously ineffective in predicting the behavior of even the very same people who filled out the survey or came to the focus group, let alone of others like them. When you take a leap and gather feedback, don't take all the feedback literally or at face value. Instead, take some time to reflect on and interpret it.

Let's say you create a parenting workshop and deliver it to a small pilot group. You get the feedback that pilot parents felt the workshop was too intensive and too long. They say they want something shorter that they can digest in small bites.

Now, you've got to *interpret* that feedback. It doesn't necessarily mean that you should make the workshop shorter or slice it up into those small pieces. Some other conclusions you might draw:

- Perhaps this group wasn't your target audience. Maybe your audience is comprised of those ready for more "advanced" material or people who themselves advise others on parenting. That tells you what to experiment with next: trying the product out with those groups.
- Or perhaps you notice that when that pilot group complained about the intensity and the length of the work-

shop, they seemed exhausted. You might try incorporating more breaks, physical movement, and fun activities into the workshop to see if that makes the intensive format work better for them.

You get the idea. The connection between the feedback you receive and the changes you make as a result isn't always an obvious one. Your expertise—as a creator and a listener—plays a critical role. It's up to you to gather, synthesize, and reflect on feedback to discern what it means for your project/product/creation.

When it comes to playing bigger, brilliant women can choose the discomfort of early feedback gathering or the pain that comes when a carefully crafted and long-nurtured creation flops. It's one or the other. Early conversations with your intended audience make you feel vulnerable, but in exchange for jumping into that sandbox you receive feedback that you can utilize when you still have plenty of time to course-correct. If, instead, after months or years of vision-ing, planning, and developing you bring an untested creation into the world and then find out it *doesn't* resonate with the intended audience, you often can't course-correct—because you've run out of time, stamina, or funds, or worse, because you're just too devastated by the results to keep going.

One of my favorite leap stories comes from Helena, a new empty nester who was exploring what to do with her time and energies now that her kids were out of the house. When the time came for each woman in the Playing Big course to choose a leap and share it with the group, Helena said:

"Well, my leap is to write a list of my passions and write about why I'm passionate about them, and then choose one to commit to. I haven't been able to decide what my main focus is right now, but I have lots of ideas—too many ideas in fact. So I'm thinking this will help me move forward."

As you can imagine, I wasn't going to let her off the hook with that. Writing a list of one's passions is not a leap! In fact, it's designing at the whiteboard, assuming you have to make the perfect choice (or that you can make the perfect choice) of what direction to pursue while sitting in isolation at your desk and thinking hard about it. Classic hiding strategy! Leaping is about learning via doing—not trying to "figure it out."

I asked Helena if she'd be willing to pick one of the areas she's passionate about and jump into action on it now, before knowing if it was the "right" one. Was there one area that felt especially compelling? I asked. I had a feeling there would be, because most of the time when women tell me they don't know what they want or they are overwhelmed with options, it's because what they deep-down want scares the heck out of them. They've told themselves, *That* can't be it. It must be something else. Since they've set aside the one option that does feel right, the other hundred options feel equally interesting to them, and as a result they end up feeling confused or overwhelmed.

There *was* one area that seemed most compelling, Helena told me. She was drawn to the field of physical therapy. Then she said her next step to pursue that direction would be to get a degree in anatomy and physiology.

"What is drawing you to physical therapy?" I asked her.

Helena replied that she was passionate about helping people age better, helping people deal with the physical and emotional changes that come with aging, and putting in place behaviors that would slow the aging process. Helena's voice started to change as she talked about this: It became infused with energy and at the same time sounded calmer, more centered. I could tell that Helena had some hard-won personal lessons about aging well, but that out of fear of playing bigger right now, she'd convinced herself that the only path to sharing them was to go to school for years and then become a physical therapist.

I said to her, "It sounds to me like this passion comes from your personal experience, and that you have a point of view and some ideas to share already—is that right?"

"Well, yes," Helena said.

We decided Helena's leap would be to write an article or blog post sharing her point of view, or to hold a small, simple event for a handful of people in middle age during which she'd give a short, personal talk on the lessons she's learned about aging. She would learn a lot about her message—which she hadn't crystallized yet— and she'd learn about what aspects of that message seemed to resonate most with others.

Within a few minutes, we had a plan that got Helena playing bigger and pursuing her passions *now*—not years from now. If, down the line, she decides she also wants to pursue a degree in anatomy or physiology or get certified as a physical therapist, great, but then she'll be doing it as a way of expanding her playing bigger, not putting her playing bigger on hold.

LEAPING: A RECAP

· ·

A leap meets these six criteria:

- It gets you playing bigger now, according to what playing bigger means to you.
- It can be started and finished within one to two weeks.
- It's simple, an action that you can describe in a short phrase.
- It gets your adrenaline flowing.
- It puts you in contact with those you want to reach or influence.
- At its center, it has a learning goal—a question you can answer by doing the leap.

A leap is never:

- A decision. It's the decision + the action.
- Solitary. It puts you in contact with those you want to reach or influence.
- About sharing your work with family, friends, or mentors. It requires sharing your work with its intended audience, the people you most want to impact and serve.
- Taking a training course or enrolling in an educational experience. A leap has you sharing your gifts with the world now, not after completing a class.

Journaling Questions

....

My leap is to . . . (describe your leap in a short phrase and check it against the criteria to make sure it's a true leap!):

The time line is . . . (give yourself a deadline for the leap, or a few deadlines for the steps within it, all to be completed in less than two weeks):

The learning goal of this leap is to find out . . . :

The Big Ideas

1. The antidote to our common hiding and delaying tactics is a special kind of action called leaping.

2. A leap has you playing bigger right now, is simple, can be completed in one to two weeks, gets your adrenaline flowing, and puts you in contact with the people/audience/customers/stakeholders you want to reach through your playing bigger.

3. A leap has at its center a question—something you want to learn by doing the leap.

4. We resist leaps, because they often feel uncomfortable and scary—especially at first when we are unpracticed in them.

5. There are tremendous benefits—both psychological and tactical—to leaping: We avoid costly mistakes, learn about what will really work with our intended audience, and experience the joy and meaning that comes with playing bigger *now*.

CHAPTER 8

• • •

Communicating with Power

Listen with fresh ears to the women around you, and you'll hear some odd turns of phrase. You'll notice that much of the time their words sound like a kind of struggle—between saying something and holding back, between asserting and not being too assertive, between sharing an idea and diminishing it.

You've probably felt this struggle inside of you.

Most women I know feel great pressure—sometimes conscious, sometimes unconscious—to say what they really want to say, while also adhering to feminine norms of being "nice," ever flexible, ever conciliatory, ever calm.

As a result, there are a number of "little things" women tend to do in our speech and writing that in fact aren't little at all. They have a big impact and not a positive one. These "little things" are attempts to walk the fine line of saying something without coming on too strong, but in fact they convey tentativeness, self-doubt, or worse, self-deprecation. Women with important messages and wise insights diminish themselves through their words—usually without knowing it.

Here are ten of those very common undermining speech habits. Which ones do you use?

1. "Just." While writing this chapter, I went in for a doctor's appointment with a younger female doctor whom I hadn't seen before. She used "just" about five times in the first five minutes of the appointment. "I know you are here for *x*, but I just need to get a few things down in your chart first, so I'm just going to ask you a few general questions." She sounded vaguely apologetic, as if she were inconveniencing me in some way when she was in fact taking a responsible approach to the appointment.

We're very fond of inserting "just" into our sentences: "I'm *just* concerned that . . ." "I *just* want to check in and see . . ." "I'm *just* wondering . . ." We do this when we feel slightly awkward or apologetic about what we have to say, when we're worried about coming on too strong, when we feel as if what we have to say has to be *just*ified. But hear how much more powerful and confident these statements sound without the "just" in them? "I'm concerned that . . ." "I want to check in and see . . ."

"Just" often shows up with "curious." "Did you do competitive research on this? I'm *just curious* whether other companies are doing something similar," you might say. When you have a question to ask (especially a bold, provocative question), you might feel the need to reassure the listener that the question has no aggressive intentions behind it. But "just curious" diminishes the import of the question and obscures your real, thoughtful reason for asking.

2. "Actually." Then there are the "actuallys." "I *actually* think . . ." "I *actually* have a question." "I *actually* disagree." "Actually" makes it sound as if you are *surprised* that you have a question or that you disagree.

3. "Kind of/Almost." "I *almost* think we should go a different direction." "I *kind of* think the report should be reorganized this way." We do this—often unconsciously—when we're uncomfortable asserting our ideas with certainty or when we're afraid of coming on too strong for others; but think about it: Can you picture any leader you admire saying to her team, "I kind of think we should . . ."?

Linguists call these sneaky little additives—words like "just," "actually," "kind of," and "almost"—hedges. Research shows that low-power and low-status people in any group use more hedges than higher-status or high-power individuals, and that, accordingly, women use hedges more than men.

4. "Sorry, but . . ." Two of my friends, who were roommates throughout graduate school, suffered from this habit. They were in prestigious professional careers—PhD students at a top university— but they found they were constantly apologizing to each other for all kinds of nonsensical reasons. So they set up a jar in their kitchen, and every time one of them said a ridiculous, reflexive "sorry" to the other, she had to pay up—a dollar in the jar.

Of course, there are times to say sorry, when you have a sincere apology to make. But many women have the habit of unconsciously apologizing for taking up space, having something to say, or asking questions: "*Sorry* to bother you, but . . ." "*Sorry* if this is a silly question, but . . ."

5. "A little bit." In presentations, I often hear women say, "I'd like to take *just a few minutes* of your time," or "I'd like to tell you *a little bit* about our new product," as if what they're about to say isn't worth much time or too many words. Of course, it's great to *be* succinct, especially in business contexts, but you can do that without the up-front qualifier of "this won't take much of your time." Hear how different it sounds to confidently say, "I'd like to tell you about our product" rather than "I'd like to tell you *just a little bit* about our product"?

6. Disclaimers. You know these: "I'm just thinking off the top of my head, but . . ." "You all have been thinking about this a lot longer than I have, but . . ." "I'm no expert, but . . ." "This is just an idea, but . . ." We do this because of conditioning to be ever humble or because we know our thinking is in progress and want others to know that too. Yet we can speak about that in ways that don't diminish ourselves. For example, "Let's do some brainstorming about this. Here are some of my thoughts." That's quite different than qualifiers that tell your listeners why what you are about to say is likely to be wrong.

7. "Does that make sense?" Many women have a well-worn habit of ending statements with "Does that make sense?" This is an attempt to reach out to the audience, check in, and find out if we were understood. That *intention* is good, but research shows that women who use this kind of question at the end of their statements are seen as less influential and less knowledgeable about their topic. It's no wonder, because when we ask, "Does that make sense?" it suggests that *we, the speaker,* think we might have been incoherent; we're not confident our thinking is clear. When you ask, "Does that make sense?" it suggests that you believe if the listeners have lots of questions or are confused, it's because *you* didn't make sense—not, for example, because you expressed complex and novel ideas that they might need to ponder for a while!

I believe this habit has a very deep root in us, that we have unconsciously internalized the stereotype that women are often irrational, babbling, unintelligent. That belief can manifest in the feeling of "I'm not making sense."

You can still honor the intention to reach across the table to your listeners and check in with them to make sure you are understood and that they are following you, but instead of asking, "Does that make sense?" ask about *them*. "How did that land *with you?*" or "What are *your* thoughts?" or "Do you have questions?" Express interest in your audience's reaction and give them the opportunity to ask questions, *without* diminishing yourself as you do so.

8. Uptalk. Uptalk is raising your pitch at the end of a statement. Think about how you'd ask a friend, "Want to go out to dinner?" Your pitch gets higher at the end of the word "dinner," because in English we raise our pitch at the conclusion of yes/no questions. When women use uptalk, raising their pitch at the end of a sentence, Valley Girl–style, their statements sound questioning, tentative. Research on uptalk shows that listeners think the uptalker is not sure what she is saying is relevant or valuable to the discussion at hand. A singsong tone is similar and can also make the speaker come across as less authoritative. Notice if you raise your tone at the end of your sentences or have a singsongy way of speaking, and practice doing it differently.

9. Rushing and piling on the words. Imagine sitting across a table listening to a woman say, "We are working hard on this, because we want to get the business up and running by 2012, specifically April 2012, which is the target date, and we are very optimistic that with the right financing we can get there, and so that is why I've been approaching different investors every day . . ." You know this type of communication: Clauses get piled on top of one another, the speaker interrupting her own thoughts with digressions. It sounds frenetic and the speaker sounds insecure.

In contrast, imagine listening to this: "We are working hard on this. We want to get the business up and running by April 2012. We're optimistic that with the right financing we can get there. I am approaching different investors every day." All that has changed is punctuation and pauses, but speaker number two sounds calm and trustworthy.

When we don't feel we have the right to take up space in a meeting or conversation, or when we're nervous, we rush and never leave a moment without words. Some theorists postulate that women also rush because they tend to be interrupted more often than men and develop the coping strategy of rushing so that they are less likely to be interrupted during pauses.

Yet pauses between sentences connote confidence. They give you time to breathe so you can stay centered and so your breath can infuse your voice with more strength and volume. They give you a moment to collect your thoughts, and critically, they also allow the listener to absorb what you are saying. Punctuate and pause.

10. Substituting a question for a statement. When we fear coming on too strong, using a question instead of a statement seems like a good idea. You might decide that saying, "I really think we need to increase the marketing budget" feels too risky, so instead you ask, "What about increasing the marketing budget?" Problem is, your colleagues aren't likely to hear an opinion (and certainly not a well thought-out opinion) in your question. Over time, women who frequently use questions instead of statements may end up being perceived as not having a clear point of view, making astute observations, or raising important points—because their ideas are always hidden as questions.

Sometimes, of course, there are strategic reasons to use a question rather than a statement: to gently introduce an idea to a group who is likely to be resistant to it, for example. But women often turn to questions rather than statements because they are avoiding conflict, visibility, and claiming power. We use questions because we have old, internalized stories—often untested in our current context—about its being dangerous or inappropriate to state our ideas definitively, and we can't see how sharing our perspective boldly and directly could hugely benefit our careers.

Undermining Speech Habits	
Hedges	"Just" "Actually" "Kind of" "Almost"
Apologies	"Sorry, but" "Just a minute" "A little bit"
Qualifying Phrases	"I'm no expert, but . . ." "I know you've all been thinking about this for a longer time than I have . . ." "I could be wrong, but . . ." "I'm just thinking off the top of my head . . ." "Does that make sense?"
Undermining Structures	Uptalk and singsongy tone Clause after clause—no "periods" in speech Substituting a question for a statement

But If I Stop Using These Speech Patterns . . .

As I worked with women on changing these speech habits, I became curious: *Why* were we talking this way? What were the roots behind these speech patterns? Was it merely "contagion"—we heard other women talking this way and conformed to what we heard? Was it the inner critic manifesting in speech patterns that reflected our self-doubts? Was it something else? I started to explore with women the deeper reasons so much qualifying was showing up in our speech, and I looked inward: When I used these kinds of speech habits, what was I feeling that caused me to do so?

What I found was this: Yes, in part we speak like this simply because of "contagion"—we hear how other girls and women talk and mimic what we think "feminine" behavior is supposed to sound and look like. In other cases, self-doubt expresses itself through these patterns in our speech. But there was one other factor causing us to undermine ourselves with our words: the "double bind"—the well-documented phenomenon that women are perceived as competent or likable, but not both. When women use these speech habits, they are often doing so in an attempt to lessen their perceived competence so that they come across as more likable.

My initial articles on this topic—simply recommending to women that they get rid of these undermining habits—didn't address the reality that many women were using these ways of speaking to navigate around the double bind. Many women felt they wouldn't be heard, or received well, without these qualifiers, undermining structures, apologies, and hedges.

One woman told me, "I work in an environment where, as a woman, I *need* to use that kind of speech to be heard. If I took away the qualifying, tentative tone, I'd be labeled a ballbuster or a bitch and no one would listen to me at all. This is how I soften my voice so that I'll be listened to." Another said, "Tara, I already do what you are advising. I don't use these softeners in my speech, and it gets me in trouble. I keep being told by my bosses that I'm too direct, too harsh, that I need to temper what I'm saying because I make people uncomfortable."

Research from psychologists Amy Cuddy, Susan Fiske, and Peter Glick has found that across all kinds of cultures and contexts, when human beings encounter a new person, they evaluate that person on two dimensions:

1. *Is this person warm? Are they trustworthy, good-natured?*
2. *Is this person competent? Are they clever and likely to be effective in achieving their aims?*

This way of sizing up strangers has an evolutionary basis. For survival, when humans encountered a new person or tribe, it was necessary for them to ask, Is this person friend or foe? (in other words, do they seem warm and friendly or not?) and, How clever is this person, which is to say, how dangerous are they likely to be as a foe, and how helpful as a friend?

Research shows that when a person is a member of a high-status group within the society, people are able to see them as both warm and competent. For example, in our culture, it's easy for white men to be viewed as both warm and competent. Members of out-groups or low-status groups, on the other hand, are generally seen as only one or the other—competent *or* warm. This is the wider context for the double bind women face: It's not just women but all stereotyped, low-power groups who are seen as either likable or effective, but not both.

The research by Cuddy, Fiske, and Glick also discusses two fascinating patterns in *how* people assess warmth and competence. First, we tend to judge "is this person warm, nice, friendly?" *in an instant,* while our assessment of their competence builds *over time.* Second, once we deem someone competent, they have to do *a number* of incompetent things for us to shift that assessment and see them as incompetent. In contrast, it takes only *one or two behaviors* that we perceive as cold or selfish in order for us to change our opinion about whether someone is trustworthy and warm or not. You can begin to see a picture of how we assess other people: a quick, intuitive assessment that looks for any cues that this person might not be nice/trustworthy/warm, and a slower assessment that looks for cues that someone is competent.

Women need to do more than our male counterparts to come across as both warm and competent. We likely need to be more deliberate about continuously conveying warmth even as we are demonstrating our competence. I don't like that this is true. I think it is terrible that women have to put in all that energy and care to do their jobs while also essentially coming across as nice the whole time they do so. It's exhausting, and it can make it very difficult to simply say what one has to say or do what one has to do. It's less true for women entrepreneurs or those who work independently. But for women working within organizations, the sad reality is we still live in a time when women who don't consistently convey that warmth don't fare very well as leaders, where their success and tenure is dependent in part on how they are liked by their superiors and their colleagues.

In this context, it is no surprise that women sometimes dumb down how competently we come across—using many of the ten speech habits discussed in this chapter—in order to seem more likable. Or we speak without these softeners and are perceived as competent but not likable. The challenge for women is to instead amp up *both* the competence and the warmth that we project.

The research also implies that we should lead with communicating warmth—since the listener makes their initial, snap judgment of that. Then, we want to keep communicating warmth but also demonstrate competence, allowing the listener to build a sense, over time, of our effectiveness.

So, how can you convey warmth, trustworthiness, friendliness? Through "bids for connection." A term coined by relationship researcher John Gottman, a bid for connection is "anything and everything designed to promote or restore a feeling of connection and solidarity between two people." We can expand this definition to include actions between one person and a team or group as well. Verbal bids for connection include making small talk at the opening and closing of a meeting, asking people about how they are doing or about what's happening in their lives, inquiring about someone's work project in a warm and friendly way, or making jokes. Many of the most powerful ways to communicate warmth are nonverbal, such as orienting the body toward the listener, smiling, nodding, mirroring the nonverbal behaviors of your audience, and using considerate gestures such as opening a door. (Although these should be used moderately; excessive nodding or smiling causes women to be perceived as less authoritative.) In other words, we convey warmth by being kind, being social, being human. It's not rocket science, but for many women there's a shift here: from navigating the double bind by diminishing what we have to say to navigating it by mindfully expressing both warmth and competence.

The unhelpful speech habits—hedges, undermining structures, apologies—are, at their root, misguided bids for connection. We say, "I haven't thought about this as much as you have, but I think . . ." because we want to stay connected to the listener rather than come across as arrogant or rude. We say, "Does that make sense?" because we want to reconnect to the listener and know they are understanding us. Yet *these* bids for connection diminish the speaker. We can start to use *positive* bids for connection that convey warmth without simultaneously diminishing our perceived competence.

Changing How You Communicate

If you know you use one or more undermining speech habits, use the following techniques to change them:

- **One at a time.** I love speaking trainer Jeanne-Marie Grumet's recommendation to change one undermining speech pattern at a time. Since these are habits, after all, it's not realistic to change many at once. Pick one habit that you'd really like to change and focus there first. For example, for a few weeks you might work on noticing when you ask a question instead of sharing a statement, and practice changing that. Then you might shift to noticing your "justs" and eliminating them.

- **Get a buddy.** Team up with a friend or colleague. Talk about your undermining habits, laugh about them together, share your commitments to which one you'll each work on first, and keep each other updated on your progress. If you pick someone with whom you work, they can tell you which patterns they hear you using—especially useful since often we are unaware of these habits in ourselves.

- **Record yourself.** Although it can feel almost unbearable to watch or listen at first, there's no replacement for seeing or hearing yourself communicate. You'll immediately notice the undermining speech habits you've been unconsciously using and know which ones to work on.

- **Keep being yourself.** Women have unique ways of communicating that are often collaborative, consensus-building, and inviting. Letting go of your unhelpful speech habits is not about adopting an authoritative communication style that doesn't sit right with you in your heart; it's about giving up the self-diminishing patterns that stem from being afraid of power or of taking up space, or from believing what your inner critic has to say.

Written Communications

Changing these habits in your written communications is just as important as changing them in your spoken ones. E-mails are a great place to start. When you are speaking, the "justs" and "actuallys" and other habits might pop out of your mouth before you know that's happening, but when you write an e-mail, you have the opportunity to pause, review, and edit.

Here's a "before and after" of an e-mail from Catherine, an artist. She's writing to follow up after submitting some of her art to a popular blog.

E-mail Version #1

Hi Marjorie—

I'm not sure if you remember me, but a few weeks ago I submitted some of my work for your Favorite Things column. I'm **just** writing now to check in and see if you've made any decisions.

I **actually** have some new pieces that I recently put up in my online gallery. Perhaps you'd like to see those too. A **little bit** of information about them: I created these paintings after spending 6 weeks hiking on the Pacific Coast, and they are inspired by my experiences there.

Thanks again for considering my work—**and sorry if** I missed some information on the time line!

Best,
Catherine

E-mail Version #2

Hi Marjorie—

I hope this finds you well. I loved today's blog post at your site. It was so creative and beautifully done. *[Opening with warmth.]*

A few weeks ago I submitted some of my work for your Favorite Things column, and I'm writing now to check in and see if you've made any decisions yet.

I also wanted to let you know about a

few new pieces of my work up in my online
gallery, inspired by my experience hiking
on the Pacific Coast. They've received a
large number of positive comments and have
been repinned over 300 times on Pinterest.

Thanks again for considering my work. I
look forward to hearing from you—

Catherine

The first version of Catherine's e-mail is full of phrases that make her sound insecure and apologetic. In version #2, Catherine has cut the diminishing phrases out, but to compensate for the lack of those "softeners," she's also more deliberately expressed warmth in both the opening and closing of her note. She also goes a little further in owning her accomplishments, sharing about the good reaction her work has been receiving.

Here's another example, from Cara, a marketing manager at a software company.

E-mail Version #1

Hi Chris and Susan—

Thanks for the meeting today. In thinking
about it more, I'm **just** not sure we are
going in the right direction with the launch
event. **I know both of you have done a lot
more research on this than I have, but** I'm
wondering: **Is the event we are planning really
going to speak to our target customers?** I do
think we need to engage other stakeholders

too, but I'm **actually** not convinced this event is the venue for that. I **almost think** this needs to feel more like the series we did in 2012—more experiential, outside of the box. **Does that make sense?**

Cara

E-mail Version #2

Hi Chris and Susan—

Thanks for a great meeting today. **I always enjoy brainstorming with you both.**

I've been reflecting on it more, and I don't think we have something yet that will speak to our target customers. My take is that this event needs to reach them, and that we can engage our other stakeholders in other ways. For this event, I think we need something more experiential and outside the box—like what we did in 2012.

I would love to hear your reactions to this. Let me know what you think.

All the best,
Cara

In version #1 of her e-mail, Cara is using qualifiers that diminish what she has to say, and she's hiding her real opinion behind a vague question. She ends up sounding tentative and passive-aggressive at the same time. In version #2, she's more direct and succinct. The qualifiers are gone, but she's also expressing more warmth—especially in her opening and closing. And she's replaced

"Does that make sense?" with the more positive "I would love to hear your reactions to this."

"Before You Hit 'Send'" E-mail Checklist

Use the "Before You Hit 'Send'" E-mail Checklist below to help you write more powerful communications. (You can grab the checklist from the web at www.taramohr.com/pbbookmaterials if you want to have a version to keep handy near your desk.)

☐ **1. Check for "shrinkers"**—words like "just," "actually," and "almost" (as in "I *just* think . . . ," "I *actually* disagree," "I *almost* want to suggest that we . . ."). Delete them!

☐ **2. Check for any unnecessary apologies**—places where you are saying sorry for no good reason or for simply taking up space on the planet. ("Sorry to bother you, but . . . ," "Sorry if this is a silly question . . .")

☐ **3. Check for any added "a little bit" or "just a minute" or "just a sec" phrases**—anything where you are implicitly suggesting what you have to say isn't worth much time or space.

☐ **4. Check for any instances of "Does that make sense?" "Am I making sense?" or "Do you know what I mean?"** Replace these questions with something like "I look forward to hearing your thoughts," or "Let me know if you have questions about this." Even if you are trying to make sure your audience understood you, find out if they have questions *without* implying that you've been incoherent.

☐ **5. Check for any undermining disclaimers:** "I'm just thinking off the top of my head, but . . . ," "I'm no expert in this, but . . . ," or "You clearly know about this more than I do, but . . ." Delete the qualifier and simply say what you have to say.

☐ **6. Check for places where you are hiding your point of view behind a question.** Instead of sharing your opinion, for example, "I think this is the wrong direction for us to take," you might have written, "Does everyone feel sure about this direction?" Use questions as replacements for more explicit statements only when it's strategic—not as a way of hiding your ideas.

☐ **7. Weave in warmth.** Include a personal, friendly, warm opening and closing. Add a little humor into your communications when appropriate. Express your interest in hearing the recipient's thoughts and response. Make bids for connection.

Journaling Questions

....

Which of the undermining speech habits do you regularly use? ("Just," "just curious," "actually," "kind of," "almost," excessive apologizing, "a little bit," "just a minute," uptalk, undermining qualifiers, substituting a question for a statement, and "does this make sense?")

What do you think are some of the reasons you use these speech habits? Some reasons to consider include habit; the influence of women around me; feeling nervous about what I have to say; concern that I'll sound too aggressive, arrogant, or bitchy; people-pleasing or conflict avoidance; or my sense of how women need to communicate within my organization.

Which undermining speech habit would you like to work on first?

What are some of the strategies for communicating warmth—verbal or nonverbal—that you could see yourself using?

The Big Ideas

1. Some of the most common ways women undermine themselves with their words include:

   - Hedges—insertions of words like "just," "actually," or "kind of."
   - Unnecessary apologies or qualifiers: "Let me tell you just a bit about . . . ," "I'd like to take a minute to tell you about . . . ," "I'm not an expert in this, but . . . ," or "You've all thought about this more than I have, but . . ."
   - Tag questions, especially "Does this make sense?" or "Am I making sense?"
   - Undermining structures like uptalk or substituting a question for a statement.

2. Many women are caught in a double bind with their communications, dumbing down how powerfully we come across in order to be perceived as more likable.

3. Instead, we can consciously convey both competence and likability by dropping undermining speech habits while amping up the warmth with which we communicate.

CHAPTER 9

• • •

Callings

For nearly thirty years, social worker Kris McBride counseled children and adolescents in the foster care system. In her late fifties, she started to feel a strong longing to improve the poorly designed laws that often had negative consequences in her clients' lives. She knew the system inside and out, and she had a point of view about what needed to change. Kris was coming up on retirement, however, and her husband was more than eager to move with her to a condo on a golf course and spend their days relaxing with friends. And Kris could think of a number of reasons to not pursue her longing—she didn't have much experience with political advocacy and she knew the system was very broken. But Kris could not shake the feeling that she was meant to do something to improve legislation that hurt foster kids.

Kris was experiencing a calling. **A calling, as we'll define it in this chapter, is a longing to address a particular need or problem in the world.** Callings are about making a contribution for the good, about in some way bringing more light and love into the world. They are a path through which we can respond to the lack and brokenness we see before us.

All the skills we've discussed—quieting the inner critic, drawing on the inner mentor, managing fear, unhooking from praise and criticism, leaping, communicating with power—can be applied to whatever kind of work you do to make a living. But they can also be applied to your callings, whether your callings happen through your job or not. Many women feel they are most truly playing big when they play big with their callings. This chapter is about how to recognize and pursue yours.

About Our Callings

Some callings are big, long-term projects. Others are smaller, shorter-term endeavors that might take a day or even just an hour. What defines a calling is not its duration or the domain in which it takes place, but the sense of passion and longing to address a particular need. All these are examples of callings:

- "I felt called to teach kindergarten and create a positive, safe environment for kids."
- "I felt called to be a companion to isolated people in their final years."
- "I felt called to create a new kind of bodywork to help people live with greater vitality."
- "I felt called to help my company develop a new product that would solve an important problem for our customers."
- "I felt called to start a tech company that helps women manage their finances and learn about investing."

- "I felt called to write young-adult science fiction novels with inspiring heroes and heroines, giving teens role models and developing their imaginations."

In one way or another, we each have experiences like this: Of the world's myriad needs, one calls out to us and says, "This. Here. This piece of what is missing in the world has something to do with you. This work is yours to do." Our callings are about our "work" in the deepest sense—but that "work" might take place in the realm of career, family, community, or our pursuits outside of those areas. Following our callings is one of the most important and fulfilling ways we can play bigger.

SOME EXAMPLES OF CALLINGS

Community callings

- Contribute to changing a specific local or global situation that needs remedying—food safety, climate change, domestic violence, or corporate corruption.
- Give time, advocacy, money, or your skills to a cause.

Career callings

- Pursue a particular career.
- Launch a business.
- Take on a new role at your organization.
- Initiate a project at work.
- Mentor someone in your field.

- Advance your field in a specific way.
- Eradicate a destructive practice in your industry.
- Create an innovation in your field or bring one to scale.
- Enrich your team or company in some way.
- Create a more humane and caring workplace.

Creative or vocational callings

- Pursue a craft or fine art.
- Start a blog or website around a passion or big idea.
- Coach a local sports team or become a mentor or "big sister."
- Form a group or community (i.e., a divorced women's support group, a gardening club, a spiritual study group).

Eight Ways to Recognize Your Callings

Callings reveal themselves through eight common patterns. You don't need to experience all eight of these (and probably won't) around any given calling, but likely, if something is a calling for you, it will show up in at least a few of these ways:

1. You feel an unusually vivid pain or frustration around the status quo of a particular issue or topic. You feel and see what's lacking in some aspect of your community, company, or industry, and it pains you. Maybe the lack of color, design, and beauty in public spaces drives you crazy. You keep wondering, How can we expect people to treat one another with decency and do good work in such harsh environments? Or perhaps you find you can't stop thinking about the inefficiencies in the medical system. You see how friends and family are not getting the quality health care they need and feel pulled to do something about it, but you work in an entirely different field and have no idea how to get started. Or perhaps many people in your town are enduring tough financial times, but one family's situation especially pains you. You wake up during the night thinking about them and feel that, somehow, you are meant to help. These are all examples of callings showing up through vivid pain or frustration with the status quo. Our callings challenge us to view our pain about the world differently—not as something uncomfortable to turn away from but as an indicator of the brokenness we're meant to help repair.

2. You see a powerful vision—vague or clear—about what could be. Sometimes, callings show up in the opposite way: through a positive vision about how things could be different. Perhaps you keep picturing that community garden and thinking about what it could do for your children's school. Or, as you go about your day, pictures of handcrafted, beautiful fabrics flash through your mind—fabrics unlike anything you've seen before. You want to bring them into the world. Or maybe a woman in your community is going through treatment for ovarian cancer. You know she loves chamber music. You imagine organizing a chamber music concert in her honor, and the idea won't leave you alone. These are all callings manifesting as visions of how some aspect of the status quo could be different.

3. You feel huge resistance. A part of you wants to run in the other direction. Our callings are often inconvenient, to say the least. They take us out of our emotional comfort zones and evoke both *pachad* and *yirah*. They may require us to speak up on issues where family, friends, colleagues, or neighbors don't agree with what we have to say. Pursuing a calling related to a significant problem in the world—violence, illness, abuse, environmental destruction—pushes us to confront what's really happening and feel the pain and sadness of it. For all these reasons, we resist our callings.

Many of us have the mistaken impression that we'll always feel in love with our callings and pursue them eagerly and with ease. The truth is the opposite: We deny and avoid our callings, sometimes for decades. The resistance feels like "I really don't want to go there." It often manifests in thoughts about how one's calling is unrealistic, that you aren't qualified, or it would be better to pursue down the line—not now.

4. You feel a sense of "this work is mine to do" or of having received an assignment. There may be no apparent reason why *you've* been assigned the calling; it may seem unrelated to your education, professional background, or personal experiences, and yet you feel the call. This sense of being called, or even assigned, is what pulls you past the resistance and into action.

5. Doing the work feels special. You feel a rare sense of meaning, rightness, and immense energy when doing the calling. Certainly, there are times when the work on a calling is hard, when challenges arise, and when your capacities are stretched to their limits. There are times when your inner critic terrorizes you or when the fear of failure rages. Yet there is also something else: When you do the work, you sometimes experience something quite magical and rare—a sense of flow, a momentum that causes you to take more consistent, bolder action than you'd normally take, and a sense of "being home" in the work itself.

6. You don't—yet—have everything you need to have to complete the task. When a calling arrives in our minds and hearts, we usually don't have what we need to complete it. We can see we're missing connections, knowledge, and resources we think we need, so we often conclude the calling isn't really meant for us. In fact, *not* having what we need at the outset is one of the telltale characteristics of a calling. The mistake is turning away from the call because of those perceived lacks. Instead, we can simply begin, and gather the resources, connections, and knowledge needed *as* we walk the journey of doing it.

7. You aren't—yet—the person you need to be to do the calling. At the outset of work on a calling, you'll sense that *you aren't the person you'd need to be* to complete the calling in your heart. Perhaps you can see that you'd need far more courage, or comfort dealing with conflict, or patience. That's not just your inner critic talking; it's *true*! You aren't the person you need to be to complete the calling—yet—but pursuing the calling will develop those lacking capacities in you. Herein lies the dual purpose of our callings: to enrich the world and to grow, in just the ways we need to grow. When we turn away from our callings, we're turning away from our customized curriculum for personal growth.

8. The journey is the reward. Most of us think along these lines:

"I want to start a philanthropy lecture series at my company; I'll feel so satisfied *when the series is up and running.*"

"I want to mentor women entrepreneurs; I'll be so happy *when I'm mentoring a few and seeing them succeed.*"

"I want to work on changing farm legislation; I'll feel amazing *when those laws finally get changed.*"

In fact, when it comes to our callings, the pot of gold is *not* at the end of the rainbow. Satisfaction doesn't come when we assume it will; it comes much *earlier*. It comes not when we complete the calling but when we give ourselves full permission to feel the calling and begin work on it in some way. If you are doing something because you love the idea of the final result but you hate *every* step of the process, what you are doing isn't a calling. (Perhaps you are doing some things you think you need to do in order to *eventually* be able to do your calling, but that's quite different than living the calling itself.) When you're doing your calling, you feel a sense of sweetness and fulfillment *as you work on it—whether you are at the beginning, the middle, or the end.*

EIGHT WAYS TO RECOGNIZE A CALLING

1. You feel an unusually **vivid pain or frustration** around the status quo of a particular issue.
2. You see a **powerful vision**—vague or clear— about what could be around some aspect of the status quo. That vision keeps coming back into your mind and keeps tugging at your heart.
3. You feel **huge resistance.** A part of you wants to run in the other direction.
4. You feel a sense of **"this work is mine to do,"** or of having received an assignment to do a particular piece of work in the world.
5. There are challenges, fears, and doubts, but when you are actually doing the calling, you feel a **rare sense of meaning and rightness.** When you do it, you tap into an immense well of energy.
6. **You don't—yet—have everything you need to have** to complete the task.

7. **You aren't—yet—the person you need to be** to complete the assignment. You'll need to develop personal qualities you don't yet have in the amounts or ways this task requires.

8. **The journey is the reward.** You enjoy the process along the way rather than feeling as if you have to "just get through" the steps to reach the end goal or final stage.

Respecting Your Callings

Typically, when a woman first begins to feel a calling, a whole host of negative thoughts comes up. "But I could never do that." "I can't even *think* about it—I have to focus on paying the bills." "I'm not qualified." "I have no experience whatsoever in that domain." "I'm too old." "I'm too young."

Why do all these thoughts arise? We're scared. And I mean, *really scared*. Our callings evoke both *pachad* and *yirah*. They require us to risk failure and criticism, to step onto a larger stage. Our callings usually ask us to move into some kind of leadership. Our callings make us emotionally vulnerable.

So we resist our callings. A calling arrives and we often immediately say back to it, "Impossible. That can't work," or "That's a nice idea, but I'm not the gal for that. Someone else—someone more qualified or experienced or smarter or braver—is needed."

I often joke with women that we need to "date" our callings, meaning, we need to treat them the same way we'd treat someone on a promising first date. If you wanted a date to go well, if you wanted to increase the likelihood that it could turn into a wonderful relationship, you'd treat the person across from you with warmth and kindness. You'd ask them questions to get to know them, and you'd listen to the answers. You'd allow time to build a connection. You wouldn't immediately play the skeptic, listing all the reasons the relationship could never work. You wouldn't say to them, "I'm not seeing how we could ever be compatible, especially twenty or thirty years down the line." Yet this is often how we respond to our callings: skeptical if not utterly pessimistic. You are in a relationship with your callings. So what kind of relationship do you want that to be?

Part of playing bigger is no longer resisting or denying our callings and instead welcoming them and pursuing them, trusting that if they showed up, they are worth listening to.

Common Objections to Our Callings

Over the years, I've learned that some common objections come up for women when they identify and contemplate pursuing their callings:

1. But I have to pay the bills. Many women feel callings that they know won't pay the bills—like teaching about climate change at the local preschool, or starting a website about making affordable meals for one's family. What I've seen again and again (and again and again) is that we don't need to do our callings forty hours a week to experience immense fulfillment from them. *Really.* Your calling probably won't demand that *it* be the way you pay your mortgage or your rent. It is simply begging you to give it some space for true expression in your life. The happiness we feel when pursuing a calling is so great, the infusion of energy so strong, that a small number of hours spent on it each week changes the way we experience every moment of our lives.

2. My calling is too big. It's unrealistic. Often, our callings are tied to some very big dreams. Women commonly hear a voice in their heads telling them those big dreams for how the world should be are naïve, idealistic, irrational. Along the way, people have probably told them their hopes and visions for what could be are just that. I think of it this way: Our callings are *grand*, our inner critics call them *grandiose*, and the work on them is all about the *granular*.

You can work on a calling in a practical, incremental way *and* let the calling live large in your heart. For me, writing this book connects to my much larger longing to see a world transformed by women's voices and women's leadership. I know this book can be only one tiny part of that transformation, but I don't need to shrink down the size of my longing because of that. Kris's real longing is to see a world in which all children grow up cherished and safe. But she's answering that call in the very practical way of helping to change her state's legislation for foster children.

3. My calling is too small, selfish, or frivolous. Sometimes women say to me, "I have an idea that matches many of the qualities of callings that you talk about, Tara. But the thing I want to do isn't feeding starving children or anything like *that*. It's kind of frivolous." Then they'll tell me about something they see as too selfish or trivial but that is absolutely a way of enriching the world. Women whose callings have to do with creating beauty—callings in interior, graphic, product, or fashion design; callings to paint, sculpt, weave, or make music—often struggle with the feeling that their callings are shallow, not serious or altruistic enough. They've internalized our cultural notion that aesthetics are something unimportant, for the privileged only. Or they are confusing beauty with materialism, assuming that any calling having to do with aesthetics is somehow materialistic. So if their calling is to make silk scarves or floral bouquets or to redesign homes, they feel as if what they are doing isn't important.

I think nothing could be further from the truth. Imagine that when everyone woke up and got out of bed, they saw something in their environment that they found to be beautiful. Imagine they went to work on a highway or in a subway car that someone had taken care to make visually uplifting. Then, imagine that wherever they worked was a pleasing, soothing environment. Wouldn't that lead us to be much less stressed and therefore more mindful, kind, and even less aggressive? Beauty calms us and inspires us. If you have a calling that has to do with bringing beauty into the world in some way, it's not frivolous. It deserves your respect.

4. But I'm not an expert at that. Quite often, women convince themselves they aren't expert enough to pursue their callings, that they'd have to be experts on the topic at hand to make a valuable contribution. Immeasurable contributions are lost because many women think traditional expertise is the only kind of legitimate qualification to pursue callings. We usually don't hold that belief when it applies to *other* people—we are thrilled to listen to someone share an insightful perspective based on their personal experience or their exploration of a topic that's new to them; but for ourselves? We think we don't know enough.

Funny how the guys don't seem to get so worried about this expert thing. My friend Sarah Milstein runs major business and tech conferences in Silicon Valley. When she's planning her speaker lineup, Sarah does her homework: She invites someone to speak only when they have deep experience or a unique perspective on the topic. When she calls to invite women to speak, they often reply that they aren't qualified enough. Since she's passionate about getting more women on her conference stages, she spends time in conversation with them, helping them to see the value of their experience. At the same time, she's found, dozens of men apply to present about topics they are far from experts on—sometimes on topics they've been doing work on for just a few months or something they read about just a few weeks before! The research backs this up. Multiple studies have found that, as compared to men, women hold themselves to a higher threshold of certainty before they offer an opinion. They are much more likely to think they don't know the answer to a question on a quiz or poll, even though if the "I don't know" option is taken away and they are forced to respond, they perform equally to their male counterparts.

Jeena Cho, author of *The Anxious Lawyer,* grappled with "but I'm not an expert" thoughts when it came to her calling. A San Francisco bankruptcy attorney and a practitioner of mindfulness meditation, Jeena explains, "Having a meditation practice allows me to build up my resilience so that I can listen to my clients' issues with compassion yet not lose myself in their suffering. I also feel more focused so that I can help develop strategies, from the legal perspective, that will solve their problems." After experiencing these effects of meditation on her own law practice, Jeena felt a calling to bring mindfulness meditation to other lawyers. The idea of spreading meditation throughout the legal world just wouldn't leave her alone.

And yet, when she was approached by *Lawyerist* magazine to be interviewed on the subject, her inner critic kept saying, "But you don't know enough." Jeena explained, "I was literally poring over a dozen books on mindfulness so I could properly educate myself, despite the fact that I've been meditating since the age of twenty-one and have gone through two eight-week courses on top of numerous retreats."

Jeena was making two mistakes. First, she was underestimating the level of expertise she *did* have. Second, she was assuming she had to be an "expert" in the traditional sense to make a valuable contribution. Jeena wasn't a conventional expert on meditation, but she was a practicing lawyer and meditation practitioner. Really, who would be better to teach mindfulness to lawyers—Jeena or a conventional expert?

Jeena was what I call a "survivor" or "insider" when it came to her topic. Survivors or insiders have lived the experience the experts study. Survivors often have insights that the experts don't. They frequently bring forward neglected perspectives and a reality check on the experts' take. They have the power to inspire, not just to inform, and they tend to bring a greater sense of passion and compassion to the work at hand. Many women aren't experts in the area of their calling, but they are survivors or insiders.

Jeena explained, "After your workshop, I decided I was expert enough. It became clear to me that all I have to do is tell *my* truth. As soon as I came home, I sat down, took a few deep breaths, and tackled all the questions in the interview. I took a few more deep breaths and hit 'Send.' The article has been shared widely on the Web, and as a result of it, I connected with a lawyer I really admire and I received a lunch request with a well-known mindfulness teacher. To top it off I was invited to come and speak to the students at the University of San Francisco School of Law." Later, Jeena shared with me that six months after the article was published, she connected with the chief editor at the American Bar Association and is now writing a book on mindfulness for lawyers, *The Anxious Lawyer*.

Jeena learned what many women learn as they step into sharing their unique survivor or insider perspective: What they have to share is more than enough. The contribution they make is all the more unique, all the more potent because they have a personal story to share rather than the official experts' take.

Other women are what I call "cross-trainers" when it comes to their callings. Cross-trainers are people who have expertise in one field and apply that expertise, that lens, to a new field. It's the physicist who feels a calling to take a look at a problem in medicine, bringing the lens of her experience with physics. It's a woman taking what she's learned during a career as a marketing manager and applying it to fund-raising. It's the family therapist who feels a calling to apply that knowledge to helping people fix dysfunctional teams at work. Cross-trainers often see the blind spots of the conventional thinking in the field they've turned their attention to. They add tremendous value to their new field by bringing in novel tools, questions, paradigms, and ways of working.

Certainly, experts make extremely valuable contributions to their fields: They have broad and deep knowledge and the benefit of connections to other experts on the same topic. But they can also get stuck in inside-the-box thinking and orthodoxies of their fields. They can become distracted by politics or debates about minutiae. The expert perspective has assets and liabilities and can provide only part of what needs to be said or created on any given topic. Being a survivor or a cross-trainer is qualification enough to share your voice.

We can each ask ourselves, Based on my background and my life experience, what is my role in the ecosystem around this topic?

What is my slice of the truth to tell? What is my right piece to add to the mosaic? What is the contribution *I* am uniquely qualified to make?

Your Big Callings

So many of us get stuck looking for our one big calling or life purpose. When we think something was "it" and then our passion fades, we end up confused and disappointed. Or when we feel pulled between two callings, we think we have to choose just one. Or we get stuck waiting for the one be-all-end-all epiphany answer to the question "What's my calling?"

Callings, as we've talked about them in this chapter, offer a different paradigm. We receive *many callings* over a lifetime. They begin and end. Often, we'll be pursuing more than one calling at a given time—perhaps one in the realm of our careers or one in our communities. If the old (not so helpful) question was "What is my purpose?" or "What's my calling?" the new question is "What calling or callings are showing up in my life right now?"

And yet, while there is this multiplicity and diversity across our callings, if you look at the many callings you've felt in your lifetime, you'll see some threads and themes. Those connections aren't always obvious. In Carol's callings, for example, a connecting thread of "supporting the underdog" showed up in a childhood passion to fight the bullies at school, and later pursuits tutoring immigrants learning English, and then consulting start-up companies to help them gain market share against larger competitors. All these callings looked very different on the surface, but they all came from Carol's same fundamental, recurring pull to support the underdog.

Sonia noticed that many of her callings had to do with healing. That theme had shown up in a calling to work on helping oceans "heal" from oil spills in her career as a fund-raiser and in callings to help elderly patients heal from surgeries in her volunteer work.

My callings share these big, recurring themes:

- **Restoring women's voices where they are missing.** I've done this in many different ways—changing my school's English curriculum to include more books by women, later creating an anthology of women's writings, and today helping women do the inner work required to play bigger.
- **Creating community.** Among my friends, I'm often the one who says things like, "What if we got together once a week and started coworking at each other's homes?" Or, "Let's start a women's dinner group." I often feel calls to create beautiful holiday and birthday parties and to organize women's circles of various kinds. This calling shows up in my personal life, in what I create among my friends, and also in my work, which now often involves bringing together live and virtual communities of women.
- **Advancing the value of compassion** through the spiritual side of my work and in the callings I feel to work for peace and justice system reform.

The threads and themes that show up again and again in our diverse callings point us to our larger, lifelong callings. When you have a sense of your big callings, your playing big gets more expansive and more coherent, more focused, all at once.

Our callings determine an important aspect of what playing big looks like for each of us. Turn away from your callings and you can have success, money, status, acclaim—but you won't have true playing big because you'll know you copped out on your real dreams for how you most wanted to contribute to our world.

Journaling Questions

. . . .

What callings have you received in the past?

What has been your relationship to your callings in the past—fear, avoidance, denial, love, delight?

How has the dynamic of trusting and not trusting your callings played out in your life so far?

What callings have you heeded? What did that feel like, and what were the results?

What callings have you ignored? What did that feel like, and what were the results?

What roadblocks or objections commonly come up for you in reaction to your callings?

What callings are you receiving right now? (Review the qualities of a calling on page 208–209 to help you think about this.)

How does your calling look or feel different when you remember that feeling resistance, not having what you need to do the calling, and not being who you'd need to be to do it are all telltale signs of a calling?

What are the big themes across your callings? List the callings you feel now and, to the extent that you can remember, the calls you felt through your lifetime—whether you followed those calls or not. What themes— obvious or subtle—show up? What do these themes and threads tell you about your "big callings" and the work you are meant to do?

The Big Ideas

1. A calling is an inner sense of longing or inspiration to fill a particular need in the world.

2. We all receive callings. Listening to and respecting those callings is one of our most important tasks.

3. Callings tend to show up as a vivid pain or frustration about some aspect of the status quo or a vision of what could be.

4. With a calling, we often feel a sense of having received an assignment, rather than of choosing it.

5. We resist our callings.

6. At the outset of a calling, we never have what we'd need to have to complete the calling, and we aren't who we'd need to be to complete the calling.

7. Our callings have a dual purpose—to grow us and heal the world.

CHAPTER 10

• • •

Let It Be Easy

Two women, each with a similar dream: Madeline made beautiful ceramics and wanted to start selling her work. Caitlin made unusual jewelry that her friends and family loved, and she too wanted to start a business so that she could pursue her creative passion full-time. Madeline took a few classes on entrepreneurship and read some books to get a sense of how she might begin. Then she did her best to work on her business before or after her day job as a physician's assistant. When I met her, she hadn't made much progress. "I'm just lazy," she said. "I really need more self-discipline. Can you help me get better with that?"

Caitlin approached starting a business differently. She knew she might procrastinate on moving forward, so she told a friend about her goal and asked if she could "report in" on her progress every week. She noticed many of the people in her life—friends and family—were skeptical that her business would succeed, so she connected with other aspiring woman entrepreneurs who had more positive attitudes about it. She thought about what would be the easiest way to start selling her work and realized it was simply to approach some local store owners she knew personally. Within a few months, she was selling her jewelry to a couple of retailers in her area and was creating a website.

The core difference in their approaches was this: Madeline relied on "self-discipline" as a way to stay motivated. Caitlin never expected self-discipline or passion to be enough. She put in place a number of supports to help her take action consistently, day after day. In this chapter, we'll explore this second approach. Unrelenting self-compassion. Wise planning. Sustainable action. That's what this chapter is all about.

The ideas that follow may challenge you, especially if you have a tendency toward martyrdom and workaholism, because this approach is all about letting the process of accomplishing your most important goals be *easy*. For so many of us—myself included—it's radical to consider that major behavioral change or significant achievements could happen not because of one's fierce will, struggle, and hard work but because we support ourselves so wisely and fully that change happens with ease.

Learning a New Way

From my very early years, I was an emotional overeater. Some years my weight was normal; some years I was a heavy kid. By the time I was twelve years old, I was very familiar with the dieting mentality, a stance that, at its core, was this: "I will control my appetite, my eating, and my weight out of sheer will. If I want it bad enough, if I just have enough self-discipline, I can do this. And if I can't, that means I'm weak and uncommitted and there is something wrong with me."

Throughout my childhood and teen years, I tried many diets—some of the commercial ones, some I made up on my own. I hoped to trim and reshape my body so that it looked more like those of the skinny girls at school and the pictures I saw in magazines.

When the diets failed, or when I failed to keep following them, I'd feel hopeless. It didn't occur to me that the problem might be with the dieting plan or with dieting itself. The only possibility I could see was that something was wrong with *me*, so I'd double-down and try the whole thing over again.

As you can imagine, this produced terrible results—cycles of hungry restriction followed by out-of-control eating, a powerful sugar addiction, and years of wasted time. It certainly got in the way of my playing big, as my energy went toward striving to lose weight or fretting about my size. Many, many opportunities were missed, not to mention many parts of childhood—from summer camp to swim parties.

In my midtwenties, though, I stopped eating the foods that were problematic for me—sugar, wheat, other refined carbohydrates—and have happily stayed away from them for what is now over a decade. I fell into a much healthier relationship with eating, weight, and my body, and, most important, I became free from emotional overeating.

What caused such dramatic change? Contrary to what our conventional narrative about behavior change would say, *making and then sustaining those changes year after year had nothing to do with self-discipline or willpower.* And, contrary to what we might expect, after the initial weeks, the changes didn't feel difficult. They didn't take iron will or great sacrifice.

So what made the difference? First, I changed my goal. I changed my aim from altering my body to living free of the suffering that came with emotional overeating. I became motivated not by self-criticism or wanting to change how I was *seen*, but by tender friendship with myself and wanting to change how I *felt*. I found compassion for all the pain I'd been through with food and tapped into a part of me that saw myself as deserving something better than all that pain. Those kinder-to-myself motivations turned out to be not "soft" or vague, but very potent.

There was a second important factor that enabled change to happen easily. I put in place all kinds of supports that made this major behavior shift *doable*: I got connected to people who had similar struggles. I amped up the tools I used for coping with my emotions so that I wouldn't turn to food for stress relief or emotional comfort, adding in more journaling, phone calls with friends, and, for a while, a support group. I made more time for sleep because I realized I turned to sugar for energy when I really just needed to put my head on a pillow. I talked to my husband, and in the early stages of my new way of eating, we got all the food that was problematic for me out of the house. For some time, I wrote down what I ate daily and sent it off to a support person so that there was some accountability and transparency around what I was eating. Perhaps that sounds like a cumbersome to-do list to you, but to me, now and at the time, it sounds like a sturdy scaffolding within which I could thrive and within which a lifelong compulsion could simply and easily fade out of my life.

The whole experience surprised me. Like most of us, I'd come to think that we achieve through drive, through willpower, through self-discipline. What I learned is that I change not through those things but by (1) having a loving-to-myself goal, not a "should" goal or an inner critic–driven goal, and (2) putting in place an abundance of practical supports that make the change truly doable.

Now, whenever I try to make a shift in my life, I think about these two factors: Have I chosen that right goal, a goal that truly resonates with and inspires me, one that comes from a spirit of self-care and not of perfectionism or self-criticism? If yes, then how can I truly set myself up for success in achieving that goal, with resources and aids that make it easy for me to take action consistently?

Research shows that trying to motivate ourselves out of fear, guilt, and shame simply doesn't work, and that in fact, being compassionate with ourselves is much more likely to cause us to act in alignment with our intentions. Psychologist Kelly McGonigal from the Stanford University School of Medicine writes in *The Willpower Instinct*:

> "My students commonly argue that if they are easy on themselves—that is, if they don't focus on their failures, criticize themselves when they don't live up to their high standards, or threaten themselves with horrible consequences if they don't improve—they will slide into sloth. They believe that they need a stern voice in their head controlling their appetites, their instincts, and their weaknesses. They fear that if they give up this inner dictator and critic, they will have no self-control at all. . . . If you think the key to greater willpower is being harder on yourself, you are not alone. But you are wrong. Study after study shows that self-criticism is consistently associated with less motivation and worse self-control. . . . In contrast, self-compassion—being supportive and kind to yourself, especially in the face of stress and failure—is associated with more motivation and better self-control."

There's No Such Thing as Self-Discipline

I want to ask you to consider a provocative idea: that there is no such thing as an innate quality of "self-discipline" or "willpower."

The American Psychological Association found that Americans regularly cite lack of willpower as the main cause for not accomplishing positive lifestyle changes. Given that so many of us feel we lack willpower, it seems reasonable to consider that perhaps the problem isn't our individual failings, but our notion of this remarkable willpower we're supposed to have.

We certainly *think* we see self-discipline in others. So-and-so who blogs consistently every morning. So-and-so who trains for marathons while working long hours at her job. So-and-so who persists in finding a market for her new business even when it gets really tough.

They all have great self-discipline, right? I no longer think so, because whenever I've had the opportunity to get a closer look at the people I thought of as having remarkable self-discipline, I found they were each driven by something different. For one of my friends who is a marathon runner, authentic passion for running plus a running group she loves are the drivers that keep her doing it every day, even when it's hard. But another friend of mine runs daily because she feels terrified of gaining weight and uncomfortable with her body. They both look self-disciplined from the outside, but in fact one is taking action out of compulsion and shame, and the other is taking action because she's well supported and loves what she's doing. When we talk about self-discipline, we tend to mean that special something that allows us to take an action even when it's really hard. "Self-discipline" is an umbrella term we use to describe an extremely wide diversity of motivations that result in consistent action.

The original meaning of the word "discipline" was "to instruct" or "to train." It came from the root word "disciple"—from the student-and-teacher relationship. In other words, the notion of disciplining originated in situations where there was *a clear authority figure (the instructor) who had authority over subordinates (disciples).* Along the way, that idea began to be applied within the self, as if there were one part of the psyche that could instruct the rest. That's a lovely idea, but no one checked to see if it was true. It is not. Neuroscientists now know there is no "executive" part of the brain that has absolute authority over the others. Various parts of the brain with different priorities and roles often fire simultaneously, and which part wins out depends on our innate biology and the specifics of the circumstances, not on an aspect of character called "self-discipline" or "willpower."

I've come to know, in my own life, and in the lives of the women I work with, that where we think we need more self-discipline, we usually need more self-love—not just self-love as an attitude, *but self-love manifested through the routines and rituals that we set up to enable the changes we desire to happen naturally and with ease.*

Ways to Let It Be Easy

So let's talk about what that looks like, the routines and rituals that help us take action toward our playing bigger. Here are six of my favorites:

1. Set "gift-goals," not "should-goals."
2. Find champions and sources of accountability.
3. See yourself in partnership with a larger force.

4. Create a plan based on your unique strengths and resources.
5. Make it the default.
6. Compassionately investigate when you get stuck.

Set Gift-Goals, Not Should-Goals

Often, when I'm working with a woman who is having trouble moving forward, we discover the problem is that she's set the wrong goal. Olivia, an acupuncturist, was eager to develop a larger clientele. She'd read that blogging was a great way for small-business owners to do that and had made a plan to blog weekly about health topics, posting on her website and sending out the articles to her mailing list. Yet she found she was procrastinating on writing articles and rarely published any. When we talked about it, we discovered that having a blog wasn't *actually* exciting or compelling to Olivia. It was what I call a "should-goal"—a goal set out of a sense of "should" rather than out of authentic interest. We talked about what Olivia really wanted—a thriving practice helping moms take better care of themselves. I asked Olivia what kind of plan she could create for her marketing that wouldn't feel like a "should," but instead like a real gift to herself. She replied she loved being face-to-face with her clients and that doing small workshops or house parties would feel like a truly enjoyable way to grow her practice. She resolved to do one small event a month. Olivia had moved from a "should-goal" to a "gift-goal."

Gift-goals feel as joyful to pursue as to achieve. Gift-goals reflect our callings and unique paths—they don't come from the pressures of society, culture, company, friends, or family. We tend to feel burdened, trapped, or sad when pursuing should-goals, and we can almost never sustain motivation for them. We often have to push toward our should-goals. Gift-goals have a magnetic pull on us because they are an expression of what we truly desire.

Here are a few examples of women's should-goals, and the corresponding gift-goals they developed when they tuned into what aspect of the goal actually felt like an authentic gift to themselves:

Should-Goal	Gift-Goal
Get the body of a fitness trainer.	Move every day to increase my own quality of life, sense of alertness, and overall health.
Clean up that horribly messy house!	Keep the house organized enough that it supports the kind of serenity I want every day.
Make partner at the law firm.	Move into a professional leadership role that I find fulfilling and that meets my financial needs well.

Can everything we work toward feel like a gift to ourselves? Aren't some things annoying or boring to do, but essential parts of living a responsible life? My experience is that many goals that feel mundane or unappealing, like saving up a certain amount of money, for example, can be should-goals or gift-goals, *depending on how you frame them to yourself.* "Get my finances together" might be an unsustainable should-goal if it's rooted in a sense of shame and self-criticism, whereas "give myself financial security so I have the peace of mind I want for myself" might feel more like a gift-goal.

Find Allies and Champions

Once you've laid the foundation of having a gift-goal, you can begin to ask yourself, What kinds of interpersonal support would make it easy to achieve that?

When I was training to become a coach, a few other woman students in the program invited me to join them for a monthly dinner. Each was in the midst of an important life and professional transition. Like them, I was going through, or at least hoping to go through, a metamorphosis—rediscovering my creative self, leaving my social sector career amid vehement protests from several people in my life, accepting my desire to work in the personal-growth world, and taking the first steps to doing so.

This group of three other women were my champions as I made that transition, and I was theirs. The most important quality in a champion is simply this: They can see the future that hasn't arrived yet. These women saw the just-emerging me, not only the current me or past expression of me. They thought the vision I had in mind for my new career was totally achievable—if not inevitable. The way they held that vision as doable, and even destined, helped me believe it could come into being.

I was surprised that I didn't need a lot of time with them to be affected by their faith in me—just a few hours a month was more than enough. And the relationships didn't need to be perfect. There were tiffs and rocky patches. When hurt feelings couldn't be resolved, the group ended in an abrupt, painful way. Champions don't need to be superhuman; they simply need to serve that nurturing, supportive role—for a time, until it's time for everyone to move on.

Who are the champions who have supported you? Teachers, friends, grandparents, mentors? Might any of them be someone you can call on for support now? When women tell me they don't have champions in their lives, which, sadly, is quite common, first I ask them to look a little harder. Sometimes we put up blinders to the champions in our midst—we don't see or take in the support that's in front of us. And if women still feel sure there are no potential champions in their lives, I ask them to start being a champion for the dreams of some special people. As we champion others, we find our way to mutually empowering relationships.

Often, in addition to champions, we need sources of accountability. When there's a difficult e-mail I have to write or a difficult phone conversation to have, I often check in with a friend who lives across the country, tell her what I need to do, and that I'll call her when it's done. She does the same with me. We move forward on things we'd otherwise endlessly avoid. Over the years, I've learned when I'm accountable to someone, *wow, do I behave differently*— consistent action happens, resistance is overcome, behavior patterns change. What kind of accountability to others might aid you in making steady progress toward your most important aspirations?

See Yourself in Partnership with a Larger Force

Along with champions and sources of accountability, there's a third kind of support that we can draw on, one more spiritual in nature: seeing yourself as in partnership with a force much larger than you. I often ask women to consider, "What larger force or energy could you see yourself as working in alignment with?" Perhaps it's the force of Love or Kindness, of Renewal or Connection. Ivy, a young woman who teaches at a nonprofit that serves kids with learning disabilities, sees herself as working in partnership with the larger force of Learning. Jenna, a choreographer, sees herself as working in partnership with the great force of Creativity. Imagining themselves supported in this way, they find motivation when it wanes and courage when they feel afraid.

What larger force do you feel would be supportive of—even thrilled about—what you are bringing into the world? What force could you come to see yourself as working in partnership with? How different does your work feel if you see yourself walking hand in hand with that larger force?

Create a Plan Based on Your Unique Strengths and Resources

Amy was excited to start working again after taking off several years while her kids were young. Her first step was going to be to write up her résumé (a task she was not looking forward to, to put it mildly) and send it off to a few local companies. I asked her, What if she approached the goal of returning to work differently? What if we used a strengths-based planning approach? Instead of starting her process with that résumé rewrite, we'd start by brainstorming all the resources and strengths she had that might help her reenter the workforce. Then we would create an approach based on those assets.

Amy's list of available resources and strengths looked like this:

- A woman in my book club who is a career counselor and who might be willing to help
- My sister-in-law, who works at one of the companies I'm interested in, and my neighbor, who works at another
- My skills as a communicator, project manager, and group facilitator
- My deep knowledge of the local community

- The free time I have during my kids' school days to devote to the job search process
- The access I have to all the resources at our library and online

Amy even added to the list some personal qualities:

- Good health
- Patience
- An open mind about the wide range of opportunities that could be a good fit

Once Amy had all this in front of her, she felt a rush of energy. Because she could see what she had going for her, she felt more confident. Her plan also changed. Instead of starting with the dreaded résumé task, Amy kicked off her process by meeting with some of the relevant connections she already had. She took advantage of the time she had to do research and informational interviews—a major resource she hadn't seen as such before.

Whatever you are looking to achieve, what strengths and resources are already present in your life that could help you? What would it look like if your plan was based around these?

Make It the Default

A host of studies has shown that our behavior is dramatically impacted by what is set up as the default mode—what we do automatically. In Germany, where people have to opt in to being organ donors, 12 percent of the population opts in. In Austria, people are automatically categorized as organ donors, per the public policy, and have to *opt out* if they so desire. Only 1 percent of the population does so. Another study found that when new employees were asked to opt in to a retirement plan, only 20 percent did so over the following three months. When the company made enrollment in a plan the default and people had to opt out, 90 percent chose to remain enrolled. Major decisions we'd expect people to consider carefully are significantly impacted by whatever is set up as the default. The question for all of us is, How can we make the behaviors we want to practice be our default mode, rather than something we have to decide to do? For example, if one of your gift-goals is playing live music, set a weekly date and time with some other musicians, rather than relying on yourself to choose to play each week.

If you can't make your desired action the default, try to at least make it super convenient. In a study about food choices, researchers found that people chose healthy options more readily if those options were listed on the first page of a restaurant menu—in other words, digging for those healthy items was too inconvenient for many people! As McGonigal reminds us, we want to set up plans for action that work for "the most exhausted version of ourselves"— not an idealized version of ourselves.

Compassionately Investigate When You Get Stuck

As I was writing this chapter, a woman at one of my talks raised her hand and asked, "But I mean, what if you are just stuck on your couch, doing nothing day after day? Isn't there a place for saying to yourself, 'C'mon, you lazy bum, it's time to get off your ass and do something'?" Her tone was harsh, self-hating. I told her I'd rather she ask herself, "Honey, what's going on? Why are you on the couch?" and listen to the answer. I asked her to trust that there is always a good and real reason for our inaction.

Whenever I talk with a woman who isn't moving forward to-ward her playing bigger aspirations, we discover a very good reason why she's stuck. Sometimes it's that she was trying to force herself into pursuing a goal that didn't truly resonate with her, and—thank goodness—something in her just wouldn't let her sell out. Or she was paralyzed by fears that hadn't been acknowledged or dealt with. Or she just hadn't given herself enough social support to enable the motivation to win out against the resistance. Or she was depleted from years of unsustainable ways of working and living and needed to restore herself before embarking on a new endeavor. There is al-ways, always a very real reason for the stuckness—it's never about "laziness" or "lack of self-discipline."

Of course, in any pursuit, there will be times of veering off course, periods when we've lost motivation, gotten distracted with other things in our lives, or simply become stuck. In those moments, it's easy to beat ourselves up, let the inner critic take the reins, and declare failure. The alternative is compassionate investigation of what is really going on. That simply means asking ourselves, with kind-ness, "Honey, what's the issue here, what's the stumbling block, and what do you need to move past it?" Then we need to listen to and act on the answer.

I hope you can begin to see the full picture here—a new, more compassionate and self-supportive way of going about working toward your goals. First, make sure your aim is a gift-goal, that it is truly resonant for you and comes from a spirit of self-care, not self-criticism. Then, put in place supports to help action happen: cham-pions, sources of accountability, a sense of yourself in partnership with a larger force, systems that make your desired action the de-fault, and a plan based on your unique strengths.

Journaling Questions

....

Gift-goals: Use one or more of these journaling prompts to help you generate ideas about what gift-goals might look like for you.

- *What could you bring into your life that would give you huge delight and joy?*
- *What goals feel like giving yourself a big, important gift— the gift of fulfillment?*
- *Putting all perfectionism, people-pleasing, "shoulds," and self-critiques aside, what do you really want to create in your life and work?*
- *What is calling you right now? (Use the qualities of a calling on page 208–209 to help you find out.)*
- *Close your eyes and picture yourself as a young child. See yourself in a childhood scene. Spend a few minutes with your childhood self and then ask him or her, What projects or activities would you like to see me pursue this year?*
- *Check in with your inner mentor. Ask her, What projects and activities would you like to see me pursue this year?*

- *What are the dreams and longings that your fears or inner critic won't allow you to even consider?*

Use your writing from the questions above to identify one gift-goal to continue working with as you answer the questions below.

Many women find they've set goals that have some "gift" elements and some "should" elements. If that's the case for you, do some journaling to pull the strands apart. How can you alter your goals or the way you are working on them to leave the "should" element aside and give it more of a gift-goal feeling?

Partnership with a larger force: What larger force for good do you think would applaud what you are doing, be aligned with what you are doing, be on your side? What greater force are you in partnership with as you work on this gift-goal?

Strengths-based planning: Brainstorm for five minutes about the resources, strengths, and assets you have already that can help you achieve your gift-goal, including all the following:

- *People/relationships/connections*
- *Information*
- *Educational opportunities*
- *Time*
- *Money*
- *Energy*
- *Communities or groups*
- *Personal talents or strengths*
- *Expertise and background*

Don't worry about getting the best ideas down or evaluating them now. Simply keep your pen moving on the page. Go for quantity of ideas, not quality. You can always go back after and select the best ones. If you get stuck and have trouble generating a list of resources, invite a friend or two to brainstorm with you. They'll be able to see resources that you can't.

Making it the default: What are the actions you want to take regularly to realize your gift-goal, and how can you set these up as the "default"? If you can't make those actions the default, how can you make them as convenient as possible?

Champions and sources of accountability: What sources of accountability and champions would be helpful to you? Who will you feel motivated to check in with, not out of fear or guilt, but because you like celebrating successes with them and feel you can be honest with them when it's not going so well? Ask that person if they'd be willing to serve as a source of accountability for you around your goal.

What frequency and format of check-ins with your accountability person would be most powerful in helping you take consistent action? Work with your accountability person to come up with a format that works for both of you.

How would you like this person to respond—to your successes and during the times you missed the mark? Talk about this with them so they know how to best support you.

The Big Ideas

1. We're more likely to be successful in achieving our goals if we are motivated by a spirit of self-care rather than guilt or self-criticism.

2. There's no such thing as self-discipline! What looks like self-discipline is really a wide array of motivations that result in consistent action.

3. We create sustainable action not through self-discipline or willpower, but by putting in place an abundance of supports for ourselves, such as

- Starting with a gift-goal, not a should-goal.
- Finding champions and sources of accountability.
- Designing our plans based on our individual strengths and available resources.
- Having routines that make the desired behaviors the "default mode" in our daily lives.
- Compassionately investigating what's going on when we get stuck.

CONCLUSION

• • •

Joining the Transition Team

After teaching the Playing Big course for a couple of years, I tried something new. I invited recent graduates of the program to participate for a second time, for free. It was an experiment. I thought alumnae would enrich the discussion, plus some students always had to miss portions of the course because of unanticipated schedule conflicts or life events, and I wanted them to be able to revisit the modules they'd missed.

I assumed a small group of alumnae would reenroll. What happened surprised me. About 75 percent of previous participants decided to join the course again. Many of them wrote to tell me that topics that hadn't seemed relevant to them in their first round now were critical to the challenges they were facing. They said things like, "When I started the course, I was so overwhelmed by my inner critic and fear. *Those* were the modules that really stood out for me. But now, I can really see what my callings are, and I'm ready to start taking leaps." Or they'd say, "I understood the praise and criticism stuff on one level the first time I took the course, but now I'm getting it in a much deeper way."

They told me something that I honestly hadn't realized, and that was moving to learn: The ideas in the course represented a major paradigm shift in how they approached their lives and careers, and it took real time for it all to sink in and become integrated. And, as they returned to the material, they found more and more applications for it. So if you don't feel "finished" yet with this work, know that that's just where you should be. The tools I've presented here are tools to keep using, again and again, as you continually stretch into playing bigger.

What can you expect on the road ahead? First, your self-doubt will disappear and you'll start feeling entirely confident in everything you do. *Just kidding!* In fact, the opposite is true. You can expect some *intense* inner critic flare-ups as you play bigger. As you follow your callings, speak up more, and communicate more powerfully, it will try to scare you right back into your comfort zone. You may listen to your inner critic for a while, before you remember that you have some ways to stop taking direction from it. That kind of forgetting and remembering is a part of the process. You will veer off track, but you will course-correct sooner and sooner as the tools you learned here become your habitual way of doing things.

If you continue consulting with your inner mentor, you can also expect your life to become more and more like hers. Some of the changes will be gradual, some seemingly sudden. Some subtle, some dramatic. No matter how the evolution happens, there's nothing like the joy of looking around at your life one day and realizing how far you've come in growing into that remarkable older, braver version of you.

You can expect to experience more and more *yirah*. You can

expect to be quicker to recognize *pachad* and shift out of it. You'll become less beholden to praise and criticism, but also continue to see new ways in which you get hooked by both—not just at work but in family and personal relationships as well. The work of unhooking from praise and criticism is ever deepening.

If the experiences of other women are any guide, what playing big means to you will become less and less about external markers of success and more and more an inner game. Recently, I was chatting with Allison, a member of my very first Playing Big course. She signed up because she was trying to build an interior design business after taking several years off to care for her kids. "When I started the program," she said, "playing big was about becoming a successful entrepreneur, about stepping into a new identity after being out of the workforce for so long." Allison learned to deal with her inner critic, unhook from praise and criticism, and calm her fears. Then she started making headlines—literally. She went after an opportunity to participate in a designers' showcase, and her work was so stunning that it was featured in the national design press. Over the next few years, Allison became a sought-after designer for many of Silicon Valley's most famous CEOs and tech founders.

Allison said to me, "Before Playing Big, I felt unsure of myself and my path. The end goal for me was just to build a business. I didn't imagine being in a place where I am so creatively fulfilled. But now that I am living that reality, I've found the headlines and big names are not a big deal. What means much more is that I now live with authenticity. I used to be so worried about other people's approval. I don't care anymore what other people think about me— I follow my curiosity, my interests, my passions. I live with so much more freedom."

I hear this refrain from women again and again. As a woman's relationship with her inner mentor strengthens, as her critic quiets down, as she falls in love with the feeling of *yirah* and the joy of following her callings, she often experiences a lot of outward success—promotions, raises, speaking engagements, media attention. Achieving those goals can be an important rite of passage, a stage of the journey that's all about seeing one's own capability. But then those external successes become the small stuff. Playing big becomes about living with fidelity to your dreams rather than to your fears.

There's one more important thing you can expect on the road ahead: You will become a change agent. I've always thought of the work I do as having two aims. The first is the happiness of the individual woman: the fulfillment she feels as she plays bigger, the sense of self-expression and authenticity, the joy she experiences going for her callings. It's about her no longer living with the painful feeling that she's playing small. But the second purpose of this work is where my real passion lies: the well-being of our society and our planet. I believe that when women play bigger, they change the world for the better, and—more precisely—they bring forward what is missing.

What I've seen over the past few years is that when women truly apply the Playing Big tools—when they go deep with inner critic, inner mentor, fear, and unhooking work—they don't just become successful within the systems as they are. They change those systems. They call out the failings of the status quo. They bring forward a more enlightened, humane way. And they do this in diverse ways, some making change within existing organizations, others through entrepreneurial ventures, and others through activism or community involvement.

It's time that we shifted the women's movement paradigm, from one of *participation* to one of *transformation*. For women, this moment in history is like no other. In the developed world, we have on paper equal access **to participate** in positions of power. We can enroll in higher education. We can participate in professional life. We can hold political office. We can own property and financial assets. Yet more and more women are finding that they want more than equal access to participation in outdated, often harmful systems. We want **to transform** those systems to make them more just, more compassionate, more sustainable for the planet and for our families. We want to add our ideas, our alternatives, our ways of working. In other words, now that we have more power, we want to use it for good.

Being a change agent requires the kind of playing big you've learned about here: trusting the voice of your inner mentor, not your inner critic; moving forward despite your fears; letting go of attachment to praise and criticism; taking leaps; getting out of good-student mode and into a mode of leadership. It requires communicating without diminishing yourself, respecting and pursuing your callings, and supporting your aims wisely and through self-care.

Let me tell you a few of the stories of positive change that have moved me.

Margaret is a director at a major global professional services firm and a graduate of the Playing Big program. Several months after she'd finished the program, I asked her what playing big looked like for her these days. She explained to me that she'd been offered a highly coveted promotion, a role for which all her peers at the firm had competed. When Margaret "won," everyone assumed she would take the job, but she turned it down—making company history as she did so.

Why? When she was offered the promotion, Margaret was 50

percent of the way through a multiyear project she'd developed from inception. She didn't want to abandon the work or her team. She valued relationships. She valued seeing things through to the end. Plus, Margaret believed that part of what created corruption and waste in her industry were the practices around promotions: a professional workforce that greedily leapt from job to job to advance as quickly as it could, one in which employees were held accountable for their immediate results but not their long-term impact. That led to poor decisions that weren't really in the interests of people—the clients, the shareholders, the investors—who were impacted by them. Participating in that did not feel right to Margaret.

I was pregnant at the time of our conversation, and I couldn't help but think of the analogy: "So you mean the existing culture was kind of one of spreading one's seed as fast and as widely as possible, and you wanted to stay put and do a good job raising the baby you'd already birthed?"

"Exactly," she said as we laughed.

When Margaret turned down the promotion, she let people know why she did it, and she established her reputation as a leader focused on long-term impact, not merely her title. That led to some even more high-profile opportunities coming her way. Further, she started a conversation with senior leaders about the costs of the frequent promotions and employees' resulting short-term focus.

When I heard Margaret's story, I thought, Yes, this is the kind of change we'll see more and more of when women enter the corporate world and are able to act from their wisdom to change it.

Margaret is making change within a traditional institution, but of course, often women decide they need to leave an organization to play big in the way they desire. For ten years, Erica had been the assistant minister within a large church, and she was the first woman to serve in that role for the church's two-hundred-year history. Although she loved her work, she felt more and more stifled within a traditional institution and by being the younger junior female under an older, male head minister. Erica was also becoming more and more passionate about issues of sexism within the black Church and felt called to devote her energies to making change around that. She grappled with her inner critic's rant that "she'd never have another job this good" and with the fear that leaving her post as a minister was leaving God.

But the pull to enact widespread change was stronger. She took a new job in religious studies at a major university. She began to develop her own body of work—writing, speaking, and teaching about women's marginalization in the Church. Her book on the subject has just sold out of its first printing, and she is doing remarkable work galvanizing religious leaders to change long-standing practices that discriminate against women.

These women are doing what I often think of as "transition team work." The past was a world defined, designed, and led by men. The future—we hope—will be a world defined, designed, and led by women and men. The present is the transition. Those of us born into this time were born into a unique and remarkable historical moment, a moment of in between. That means you and I and all the women we know have in a sense been "hired" for a very important global transition team.

When I give a talk, I often ask each woman to turn to the woman next to her, look her in the eye, and say, "You've been hired for the transition team." And then I ask the women listening to really let that sink in. The historical moment we live in can feel so confusing. We're told things are mostly "equal" now, but the "equality" isn't translating into the results it should—like a critical mass of women in leadership, girls feeling confident about themselves and their bodies, women being physically safe walking down the street. When we understand our moment as one of a major transition that will take decades to enact, and when we see ourselves as forgers of that transition, things shift. We can focus on how we want to help move the transition forward, and we can feel less wounded and frustrated by the myriad ways the transition is not yet complete. We can also feel honored and grateful to be alive at this transitional moment and to be stewards of it.

Today women have access to participate in a public life, a professional life, and a political life that is not yet reflective of women's voices or women's ways of thinking, doing, and working. That means that as we participate in those realms, we'll often feel like outsiders, like strangers in a strange land. It's our job to not run away from that but, instead, take up our small piece of the transition team's work, sharing our ideas, our voices, our callings in a way that is authentic to us. By so doing, we'll create a more balanced, sane culture, one reflective of both men's and women's voices.

That means that whether you signed up for it or not, you will be a revolutionary. You will be a revolutionary because any woman who is being authentic in her work will bring forth ideas and ways of working that run counter to the status quo of her company, industry, community—a status quo defined by masculine values and masculine ways of working.

You don't have to intend to be a change agent. When a woman truly begins playing big according to what that means to her, she becomes one, naturally. The tools you've learned on this journey can certainly help you succeed better in traditional ways, within traditional systems. But they are most potent as tools to assist you in doing your transition team work. Let them strengthen your ability to be an agent of change.

In the minds of women around the globe lie the seeds of the solutions to climate change, poverty, violence, corporate corruption. For me, in the end, the bottom line is this: In millions of communities, organizations, companies, and families, women know what needs to be done. Playing big is doing it.

AFTERWORD

• • •

New Motherhood and Playing Big

I wrote this book while I was pregnant. It was about 9:00 A.M. on a June day when I chose a literary agent and, on the phone with her, made a plan for the months ahead. At 3:00 P.M. on that same day, I realized I was having some unusual symptoms, and at 5:00 P.M., I learned—happily—that my husband and I were expecting.

So for the past year and a half, I've been on two parallel creative paths: writing a book and growing a baby. As I write these words, my son is kicking his legs with glee as he coos at the mobile in his crib. And here I am, a new mama.

When I shared the news of my pregnancy, many of the women in my life were eager to know how motherhood would change my work. One declared, "Oh, good—maybe you'll be able to tell me how to play big and be an involved mom at the same time, because I can't figure that one out!" People were curious to know if the focus of my work would shift to motherhood, or to see how caring for a child would alter my perspective on women's career issues. Of course, all that will be an unfolding story, and I'm just at the very start of it, but I have some "beginner's mind" impressions:

FIRST, I'M STILL ME.

I missed my creative life much sooner than I thought I would into new motherhood. About two weeks into the round-the-clock breastfeeding and diaper changing, I longed to get to the keyboard and write—a blog post, some work on the book, *anything*. I loved being with my son, *and* I missed my writing. I found an unparalleled joy looking into his eyes, but that didn't mean I wanted my new mother identity to swallow my old identity. I missed my grownup, dynamic, in-the-world, let's-do-this self. Maybe it sounds silly, but that surprised me. I didn't expect that right on the other side of labor, I'd still very much be, in one way at least, the same me: a woman who loves her work in the world and is wildly grateful for that.

So in one sense, motherhood has not changed what playing big means to me, in terms of my work in the world. On the other hand, it's changed everything. My old identity is not gone, but over long nights with little sleep and days of tending to a baby's minute-by-minute needs, that identity is being resculpted into something new, something I have no words for yet.

Motherhood has also forced me into a new kind of playing big: trusting my intuition about when and how much to ramp work back up, giving myself permission to ask for help, and challenging my own "you are a bad mother because . . ." inner critic voice. In a culture that has so much judgment for the choices mothers make, motherhood demands of each woman—if she wants to keep her sanity—that she find a way to hear her own voice and trust it.

I've had moments of panic as, suddenly, the adrenaline would course through my veins and I'd think, There's no way I am going to be able to get the book done with all the pregnancy fatigue and morning sickness! I've made a huge mistake. Or I've felt guilt, thinking, Surely I would be a better mother if my attention weren't divided between the book and my baby.

After a few months, I noticed something interesting. When I had a little freak-out like these, there was never an *actual* conflict between me being a present, loving mother and me doing my work. There *was* enough time for me to write the book while pregnant. There *was* enough time for me to finish the edits when I wasn't breastfeeding or bouncing, when the baby was asleep or when my husband was caring for him. Yet something in me assumed I'd inevitably fail—at either the book or at being a good mama. Unconsciously, it seemed, I believed the "you can't have it all" narrative.

For decades, I'd heard and read so much about the career-family conflict for ambitious women that I assumed that conflict was inevitably going to descend on my life. Women a little older than me were told they *could* have it all. Many of them ended up feeling that was a stressful myth. What women my age heard were their frank, well-intentioned discussions of the hard truths around combining work and family. No news headline or conference panel on the subject I saw ever conveyed the message, "It can really all work fine together. You can exhale." I internalized the message that work-family tension was inevitable. That's a very distressing thought for a woman like me, who wants to be an involved parent, is madly in love with her child and with mothering, and who also has a very full and fulfilling professional identity.

Sheryl Sandberg writes about women "leaving before they leave"—ramping down their career aspirations *in anticipation* of partners and children who don't exist yet. I saw a similar impulse in myself, as I embraced the "it's impossible to have it all" narrative, when really, I had no *evidence* that I couldn't have the "all" that I wanted. Again and again, I had to slow myself down, take a breath, and return to my reality—a flexible job and a very involved partner—rather than the cultural story I'd been told about women, work, and family.

Outside of the panicky moments, I've felt mostly gratitude. I often think, Wow. Today, I got to feed my baby boy (about one hundred times, it seemed) *and* I got to feed the other parts of my identity—the adult woman, the creator, the one who loves to be making things happen out in the world. That's the story of working mothers we never hear about in the news, the stories of women in love with their careers, in love with their kids, and feeling good about how it's all fitting together. Their stories don't make the magazine covers. I'm ready to read the news story with the headline MOMS HAPPILY COMBINING WORK AND KIDS. EVERYTHING'S JUST FINE.

But I've noticed it's easier for me to talk with family and friends about the moments of overwhelm than the moments of contentment. It's socially acceptable for women to talk about how exhausted and overwhelmed we are or how torn we are between our career opportunities and our commitment to our kids. It's socially acceptable to talk about feeling as if we never measure up in either domain of our lives, as one constantly pulls us away from the other. But I'm not sure it's socially acceptable yet for a woman to talk about *not* feeling overwhelmed, to say she feels like she measures up. Standing in the conviction that one is a great mother and a thriving professional and saying, "Yeah, I'm resting in the goodness of both, and it's fabulous," is still transgressive—probably because when a woman declares that kind of enoughness about herself and her life, she has so much power.

MOTHERHOOD DOESN'T MEAN MARTYRDOM.

I used to hear the phrase "What is good for mom is good for baby" and think, Bullshit. That's ridiculous. There are surely lots of things that are good for baby that are extremely inconvenient for mom. And while I'm not ready to declare that what seems good for mom is *always* good for baby, every day I witness the direct connection between nourishing myself and nourishing my son. I see it when I take care of myself in little ways—being sure to eat breakfast or take a shower—and larger ways, like taking time for friends and for work, both of which nurture my soul. When I do these things I come back to mothering refreshed. When I deny myself what feeds me or try to do too much without help, I'm less of the mama I want to be.

Over the past year, I wrote *Playing Big* knowing there was a growing baby boy inside of me. It begs the question, What will the work I'm doing do for him?

The truth is I've had a secret agenda in writing this book. Yes, I want you to play bigger because it will bring you more joy and fulfillment. But more than that, I want you to play bigger because of what I believe it will do for our world.

When I look at my son's face—and he's moved on from the mobile and is sleeping in the bassinet now—and think about what I want for him, it's that safety and goodness surround him for his whole life. It's that he loves, is loved, and has days full of gratitude and wonder. I want him to work in an environment where collaboration, not competition, rules, where *everyone's* good ideas are respected, and where people are kind. I don't want him to get caught up in a race among alpha males or work in a cold culture where men are measured by their outward success and earning power. I don't want him to be seduced into doing work that strangles his soul and hurts people or the planet.

I believe that future will be realized only when leadership is equally shared by men and women, when women shape our world as much as men do. I believe that when more women are playing big, they will, together with men, create the world I want for my son and for all of us.

Tara
May 2014

ACKNOWLEDGMENTS

• • •

I am fortunate to have a wealth of thank-yous to share.

To the worldwide Playing Big program alumnae: Getting to know your stories, hearing your insights, and witnessing your trajectories of growth have taught me so much. Dozens of you also provided stories and valuable feedback along the way as I've written this book. Thank you. Keep leading.

I'm blessed with a dedicated group of brilliant women on my professional team. Thank you to Brittany Sochard, Delilah De La Rosa, Nita Apple, Teresa Aguilera, Adele Miller, and Rochelle Alejo for using your gifts to help women play bigger. And thank you to Jen Legge and Simone Montalvao for all the support.

When I began this book, I'd been blogging for about five years, and I'd gotten used to writing as a solo enterprise. I've discovered over the past months that making a good book is, by contrast, a team effort. The wisdom of Lisa DiMona, Megan Newman, Sarah Rigby, Gigi Campo, Lisa Johnson, Lindsay Gordon, and Robin

Dellabough has made this a much better book. We've truly collaborated. Thank you.

Research assistants Ali Heller from Washington University in St. Louis, Ella Washington from Northwestern University, and Laura West from Georgetown University helped me put my work in a larger context and refine my thinking. I'm grateful to each of you.

Thank you to the Coaches Training Institute for starting me on the coaching path and for the many valuable tools I learned in my training.

I live my life surrounded by a circle of remarkable women— sisters in laughter and tears, in dancing and cooking, in long conversations and silent walks. I'm so lucky that I have too many of you to thank here, but you know who you are. Special thanks to Ruth, Laura, Nicky, Rebecca, Amy, Lianne, and all the coworking ladies for being you.

There are women who have been my North Stars over the years, women who, by the path they walk and by what they embody, have helped me see new possibilities for my own life. Judith Komoroske, Tia Rich, and Sharon Cohen Anisfeld, thank you for being that for me.

Vivian, Andy, Nicole, Dov, Everett, Amanda, Gordon: Thank you for the unfailing support. I know I'm part of a very special tribe, and I'm grateful for it.

Mom and Dad, the older I get, the more I understand just how remarkable the way you raised me was. Thank you for inviting me into rich conversations from such a young age. Thank you for allowing me to move closer and closer to my true self, always encouraging me along the way. Thank you for teaching me to find home within myself, and for doing all that parents do every hour of every day, just to keep the ship afloat. (Now that I'm changing diapers, I get just how much that is.)

To my husband, Eric Ries. I couldn't ask for more love, laughter, or magic in my life each day. There's no one I love talking with, and being with, more than you. Thank you, my love.

To my son, thank you for immensely expanding my heart. I love you more than words can say. May you always play big in being true to yourself.

NOTES AND SOURCES

• • •

Chapter I: The Inner Critic

Long-term stress is correlated with a variety of health problems . . . :
T. Chandola, A. Britton, E. Brunner, H. Hemmingway, M. Malik,
M. Kumari, E. Badrick, M. Kivimaki, and M. Marmot, "Work Stress and
Coronary Heart Disease: What Are the Mechanisms?" *European Heart
Journal* 29 (2008): 640–48.

The practice is in quieting that voice . . . : Dani Shapiro, "The Creative
Descent of the Shero" (talk, En*theos Presents The Shero's School for
Revolutionaries with Jennifer Louden, September 23–28, 2013), http://
www.entheos.com/Shero-School-for-Revolutionaries/Library.

Cherry Murray is the dean . . . : Karen Kaplan, "Unmasking the Impostor,"
Nature 459 (2009): 468.

Twyla Tharp, award-winning choreographer, describes . . . : Twyla Tharp,
The Creative Habit: Learn It and Use It for Life (New York: Simon &
Schuster, 2003), 21.

She writes, "If I let them . . .": Ibid.

Chapter 2: The Voice of Inner Wisdom

As Sheryl Sandberg writes . . . : Sheryl Sandberg, *Lean In: Women, Work, and the Will to Lead* (New York: Alfred A. Knopf, 2013), 66.

Future Self Guided Visualization: This visualization was created by the Coaches Training Institute (www.thecoaches.com) and is featured in their book: Henry Kimsey-House, Karen Kimsey-House, Phillip Sandahl, and Laura Whitworth, *Co-Active Coaching: Changing Business, Transforming Lives* (Boston and London: Nicholas Brealey Publishing, 2011).

Chapter 3: A Very Old New Way of Looking at Fear

I was reading the book . . . : Alan Lew, *Be Still and Get Going: A Jewish Meditation Practice for Real Life* (New York: Little, Brown and Company, 2007).

Here's where things get fascinating . . . : Ibid. Note: Lew uses *norah* in his writings, which is the adjectival form. I have used *yirah* throughout this chapter, which is the noun form of the same word.

In a 1920 study (a study that would never be permitted today) . . . : J. Watson and R. Rayner, "Conditioned Emotional Reactions," *Journal of Experimental Psychology* 3 (1920): 1–22.

Visualize or look at calming imagery . . . : D. Tusek and R. Cwynar, "Strategies for Implementing a Guided Imagery Program to Enhance Patient Experience," *AACN Clinical Issues: Advanced Practice in Acute & Critical Care* 11 (2000): 68–76.

Use Music . . . : T. Fagen, "Music Therapy in the Treatment of Anxiety and Fear in Terminal Pediatric Patients," *Music Therapy* 2 (1982): 13–23; N. Schneider, M. Schedlowski, T. Schürmeyer, and H. Becker, "Stress Reduction through Music in Patients Undergoing Cerebral Angiography," *Neuroradiology* 43 (2001): 472–76; S. Phumdoung and M. Good, "Music Reduces Sensation and Distress of Labor Pain," *Pain Management Nursing* 4 (2003): 54–61; S. Pittman and S. Kridli, "Music Intervention and Preoperative Anxiety: An Integrative Review," *International Nursing Review* 58 (2011): 157–63.

We also learn what to fear by watching other people . . . : A. Olsson, K. Nearing, and E. Phelps, "Learning Fears by Observing Others: The Neural Systems of Social Fear Transmission," *Social Cognitive and Affective Neuroscience* 2 (2007): 3–11.

Chapter 4: Unhooking from Praise and Criticism

Relational focus. Whether by nature or nurture or both . . . : E. Lang-Takac and Z. Osterweil, "Separateness and Connectedness: Differences between the Genders," *Sex Roles* 27 (1992): 277–89; L. K. Acitelli, S. Rogers, and C. R. Knee, "The Role of Identity in the Link between Relationship Thinking and Relationship Satisfaction," *Journal of Social and Personal Relationships* 16 (1999): 591–618.

A host of studies have found that as a group, women . . . : Various research studies show that females frequently perform better in empathy, interpersonal sensitivity, and emotional recognition than do males. A study at Cambridge University, Golan, Baron-Cohen, and Hill (2006) tested the recognition of twenty complex emotions and mental states from faces and voices. They found women to be significantly better than their male counterparts at reading emotions from both faces and voices. (See O. Golan, S. Baron-Cohen, and J. Hill, "The Cambridge Mindreading [CAM] Face-Voice Battery: Testing Complex Emotion Recognition in Adults with and without Asperger Syndrome," *Journal of Autism and Developmental Disorders* 36 [2006]: 169–83.) For more information, also see:

K. Alaerts, E. Nackaerts, P. Meyns, S. P. Swinnen, and N. Wenderoth, "Action and Emotion Recognition from Point Light Displays: An Investigation of Gender Differences," *PLOS ONE* 6 (2011).

S. Baron-Cohen, S. Wheelwright, and T. Jolliffe, "Is There a 'Language of the Eyes'? Evidence from Normal Adults, and Adults with Autism or Asperger Syndrome," *Visual Cognition* 4 (1997): 311–31.

M. H. Davis, "A Multidimensional Approach to Individual Differences in Empathy," *JSAS Catalog of Selected Documents in Psychology* 10(1980): 85.

N. Eisenberg and R. Lennon, "Sex Differences in Empathy and Related Capacities," *Psychological Bulletin* 94 (1983): 100–31.

J. A. Hall, "Gender Effects in Decoding Nonverbal Cues," *Psychological Bulletin* 85 (1978): 845–57.

E. B. McClure, "A Meta-analytic Review of Sex Differences in Facial Expression Processing and Their Development in Infants, Children, and Adolescents," *Psychological Bulletin* 126 (2000): 424–53.

In a study conducted at Harvard Unviersity . . . : H. A. Elfenbein and N. Ambady, "Predicting Workplace Outcomes from the Ability to Eavesdrop on Feelings," *Journal of Applied Psychology* 87 (2002): 963–71.

Women earn 60 percent of the master's degrees . . . : U.S. Department of Education and National Center for Education Statistics, *The Condition of Education 2012* (2012).

The US Department of Education predicts . . . : Anne McDaniel, "Gender Differences in University Completion Across Europe: The Influence of Family Background and National Context," Institute for Social and Economic Research and Policy (August 2011); National Center for Education Statistics, *Projections of Education Statistics to 2021* (March 2012).

National reading tests indicate . . . : National Center for Education Statistics, *Fourth Grade Reading Highlights 2000* (2000).

Girls graduate high school with . . . : National Center for Education Statistics, *America's High School Graduates: Results of the 2009 NAEP High School Transcript Study* (2009).

Studies have found that girls spend more time preparing . . . : Allie Grasgreen, " 'The Rise of Women,' " Inside Higher Ed, February 21, 2013, http://www.insidehighered.com/news/2013/02/21/new-book-explains -why-women-outpace-men-education. See also: W-C. Mau and R. Lynn, "Gender Differences in Homework and Test Scores in Mathematics, Reading and Science at Tenth and Twelfth Grade," *Psychology, Evolution & Gender* 2 (2000): 119–25.

Studies also show that when asked to prepare . . . : R. B. Hill, "Demographic Differences in Selected Work Ethic Attributes," *Journal of Career Development* 24 (1997): 3–23.

In other words, we learn (consciously or unconsciously) . . . : M. Beirnat and K. Fuegen, "Shifting Standards and the Evaluation of Competence: Complexity in Gender-Based Judgment and Decision Making," *Journal of Social Issues* 57 (2001): 707–24.

Plus, some women feel uncomfortable . . . : V. Singh, S. Kumra, and S. Vinnicombe, "Gender and Impression Management: Playing the Promotion Game," *Journal of Business Ethics* 37 (2002): 77–89.

Women and negotiation expert Carol Frohlinger writes . . . : *The Washington Post*, "How Can Women Advance in the Workplace? Depends on Whom You Ask," March 1, 2013.

Research shows that men try to prove . . . : For more on negotiation and gender, see: Joan Williams and Rachel Dempsey, *What Works for Women at Work: Four Patterns Working Women Need to Know* (New York: NYU

Press, 2014); Sandberg, *Lean In*; Linda Babcock and Sara Laschever, *Women Don't Ask: The High Cost of Avoiding Negotiation—and Positive Strategies for Change* (New York: Bantam Books, 2007).

Research shows that women incur social costs for advocating for themselves . . . : Catalyst Report, "The Double-Bind Dilemma for Women in Leadership: Damned if You Do, Doomed if You Don't" (2007).

Chapter 8: Communicating with Power

"Actually": Sentence-initial adverbs (e.g., "Actually, there is . . . ") and adverbial phrases (e.g., "Because we have this issue . . .") have been found to mark female speech more than male speech. Speech that made use of these structures was perceived by listeners as more elaborate (and less succinct and direct) than speech that did not use sentence-initial adverbs. (See A. Mulac, J. Bradac, and P. Gibbons, "Empirical Support for the Gender-as-Culture Hypothesis: An Intercultural Analysis of Male/Female Language Differences," *Human Communication Research* 27 [January 2001]: 121–52.)

Linguists call these sneaky little additives . . . : F. Crosby and L. Nyquist, "The Female Register: An Empirical Study of Lakoff's Hypotheses," *Language in Society* 6 (December 1977): 313–22.

"Sorry, but . . .": Some research shows that women apologize more frequently than men because we have a lower threshold for what we deem an offense. (K. Schumann and M. Ross, "Why Women Apologize More Than Men: Gender Differences in Thresholds for Perceiving Offensive Behavior," *Psychological Science* 21 [September 2010]: 1649–55). Research also suggests that low-status speakers more explicitly acknowledge self-blame and expend more effort in apologizing than high-status speakers. (M. Gonzales, J. Pederson, D. Manning, and D. Wetter, "Pardon My Gaffe: Effects of Sex, Status, and Consequence Severity on Accounts," *Journal of Personality and Social Psychology* 58, no. 4 [1990]: 610–21.)

"Does that make sense?": These types of questions on the ends of statements, known as tag questions, are also a feature associated with women's speech in some research. Early research claimed women's use of tag questions signaled uncertainty (Robin Lakoff, "Language and Woman's Place," *Language in Society* 2 [1973]: 45–80), but later, more in-depth research showed that both men and women use tag questions but in different ways: Women use tag questions most often out of concern for and to connect with their audience (J. Holmes, "Functions of *You Know* in Women's and Men's Speech," *Language in Society* 15, no. 1 [1986]: 1–22). Because tag questions can also be "functional"—used to signal uncertainty—and can

signal concern for a listener, and because women's speech is judged more negatively than men's speech, women must consider how this linguistic feature may be *perceived* when they use it. A woman using tag questions too often might be judged as being uncertain of the material or too concerned for the listener, which some listeners may judge as condescending.

Uptalk is raising your pitch . . . : G. Ward and J. Hirschberg, "Implicating Uncertainty: The Pragmatics of Fall-Rise Intonation," *Language* 61 (December 1985): 747–76.

Rushing and piling on the words . . . : A study of male and female managers giving criticisms found that the genders' communication differed in several ways: As mentioned, women used more hedges and sentence-initial adverbs, but they also had longer mean length sentences. (A. Mulac, D. Seibold, and J. Farris, "Female and Male Managers' and Professionals' Criticism Giving: Differences in Language Use and Effects," *Journal of Language & Social Psychology* 19 [2000]: 389–415.) Women who use these features are perceived as less succinct in their communication patterns, making the listener work too hard to comprehend what is being said.

When we don't feel we have the right . . . : One study found interruptions to be much more skewed in mixed-gender dyads than in same-sex dyads. In same-sex dyads, both speakers tended to overlap and interrupt the same amount, while in the mixed-gender dyads, males did almost all the interrupting and overlapping. (D. Zimmerman and C. West, "Sex Roles, Interruptions and Silences in Conversation," *Amsterdam Studies in the Theory and History of Linguistic Science Series* 4 (1975): 211–36.)

Research from psychologists Amy Cuddy, Susan Fiske, and Peter Glick . . . : "Warmth and Competence as Universal Dimensions of Social Perception: The Stereotype Content Model and the BIAS Map," in M. P. Zanna, ed. *Advances in Experimental Social Psychology* 40 (2008): 61–149. (New York, NY: Academic Press). See also: A. Cuddy, P. Glick, and A. Beninger, "The Dynamics of Warmth and Competence Judgments, and Their Outcomes in Organizations," *Research in Organizational Behavior* 31 (2011): 73–98.

Chapter 9: Callings

Multiple studies have found that, as compared to men, women . . . : Allison Kopicki, "Women and the 'I Don't Know' Problem," *New York Times*, May 15, 2014; M. K. Lizotte and A. Sidman, "Explaining the Gender Gap in Political Knowledge," *Politics & Gender* 5 (2009): 127–51; A. Lusardi and O. Mitchell, "Financial Literacy Around the World: An Overview," The National Bureau of Economic Research (2011), working paper no. 17107.

Jeena Cho, author of The Anxious Lawyer . . . : Chris Bradley, "Jeena Cho on Zen Lawyering," *Lawyerist,* June 24, 2013, http://lawyerist.com/66636/interview-with-jeena-cho.

Chapter 10: Let It Be Easy

Research shows that trying to motivate ourselves . . . : In one study, female dieters who struggled with guilt around food consumption were brought into the lab and asked to eat a doughnut and to drink a full glass of water. This type of eating has been found to cause restrictive eaters to feel guilty and overindulge later. Then, half of the participants were given a self-compassion message by a researcher, including the following excerpt: "I hope you won't be hard on yourself. Everyone eats unhealthily sometimes, and everyone in this study eats this stuff, so I don't think there's any reason to feel really bad about it." The other half received no compassionate message. Then, participants were invited to sample as much or as little candy as they wanted. Those who received the self-compassion message reduced their food intake, whereas those who received no self-compassion message did not reduce their food intake to compensate for the earlier eating. (C. Adams and M. Leary, "Promoting Self-Compassionate Attitudes toward Eating among Restrictive and Guilty Eaters. *Journal of Social and Clinical Psychologyp* 26, no. 10 [2007]: 1120–44.)

Psychologist Kelly McGonigal from the Stanford University School of Medicine writes . . . : Kelly McGonigal, *The Willpower Instinct: How Self-Control Works, Why It Matters, and What You Can Do to Get More of It* (New York: Penguin Group, 2012).

The American Psychological Association found that . . . : Kirsten Weir, "What You Need to Know about Willpower: The Psychological Science of Self-Control," *American Psychological Association* (2012), http://www.apa.org/helpcenter/willpower.pdf.

In Germany, where people have to opt in . . . : Richard Thaler and Cass Sunstein, *Nudge: Improving Decisions about Health, Wealth, and Happiness* (New York: Penguin Group, 2008). For the original data, see B. Madrian and D. Shea, "The Power of Suggestion: Inertia in 401(k) Participation and Savings Behavior," *The Quarterly Journal of Economics* 126, no. 4 (2001): 1149–87.

In a study about food choices . . . : J. Downs, G. Loewenstein, and J. Wisdom, "Strategies for Promoting Healthier Food Choices," *American Economic Review: Papers and Proceedings* 99, no. 2 (2009): 159–64.

As McGonigal reminds us . . . : McGonigal, *The Willpower Instinct,* 79.

THE POWER OF READING

**Visit the Random House website and get connected with
information on all our books and authors**

EXTRACTS from our recently published books and selected backlist titles

COMPETITIONS AND PRIZE DRAWS Win signed books, audiobooks and more

AUTHOR EVENTS Find out which of our authors are on tour and where you can meet them

LATEST NEWS on bestsellers, awards and new publications

MINISITES with exclusive special features dedicated to our authors and their titles

READING GROUPS Reading guides, special features and all the information you need for your reading group

LISTEN to extracts from the latest audiobook publications

WATCH video clips of interviews and readings with our authors

RANDOM HOUSE INFORMATION including advice for writers, job vacancies and all your general queries answered

Come home to Random House